To Jonathan + P.

Happy New Year!

Hal & Ed

"Even in today's crowded market of dog-related stories, these stories stand out . . . [and] deserve to find a wide readership."

—BO BENGTSON, editor of *Dogs in Review*, *Sighthound Review*, and author of *The Whippet*

"I love this. It's like *Chicken Soup for the Soul*, with stories that are salty, spicy and sweet. Rich and filling, this book warms your heart just like Mom's comfort food. It should be read with gusto and enjoyed with relish."

—CHRIS WALKOWICZ, author of *The Perfect Match* and President Emeritus of the Dog Writers Association of America.

"The relationship between and a man and his dog is a truly special connection. This book illustrates the profound strength of that bond. An eloquent mingling of humor and reflection. I've never read anything like it."

—MONICA MORALES, NBC News

"In this rare instance, it's fair to judge a book by its cover. *Paws and Reflect* is a sweet and deeply moving paean to a love we happily dare to name: the stirring, surprising relationships between gay men and their dogs."

—ALEX MACLENNAN, author of *The Zookeeper*

"Not what I expected! It's always appealing to read stories about the friendship between man and dog, but these stories go way beyond to a land of deep devotion, uncensored humor, and fierce compassion. I cried; I laughed; I wanted more. This is a must-read, even for cat owners."

—SALLY HUXLEY, author of *The Cat Who Had Two Lives*

"*Paws and Reflect* does more than explore the bond between gay men and their dogs, it highlights the human-animal bond that so many of us are privileged to experience. I can't imagine any dog lover who couldn't relate to these stories. Sit! Stay! Read!

—DARLENE ARDEN, author of *Small Dogs, Big Hearts*

"That special bond between man and his dogs shines through and makes it abundantly clear that the mutual canine-human love and affection developed over the ages has no preferences. A truly moving and provoking collection of canine-man devotion."

—STEVEN D. GLADSTONE, ESQ., American Kennel Club, Board of Directors, class of 2009

"I really loved these stories. The mountain rescue is so dramatic. The pee-training is hysterical, and taking care of sick dogs reminded me of our Airedale, McGill, who had a similar immune disease and was similarly brave to the end. These wonderfully written stories convinced me that our precious dogs, like Mathew Phillips's 'Brandy,' are indeed touched by angels."

—REBECCA CHASE, ABC News

"Unusual, engrossing, and vivid. A marvelous collection of stories of dogs who are guides, partners, helpers and healers. It's interesting that these are not just stories about dogs, but stories about how dogs were able to help men connect with the world beyond themselves.

—JOHN CONSTANTINE, breeder, Adamis Kennel Brussels Griffons and Miniature Schnauzers, Vice-President of the American Miniature Schnauzer Club

"A wonderful collection of stories about the coupling of man and canine. These are loveable dogs and loveable men. Men who are puppy whipped, pull lame dogs in wagons, carry incontinent dogs, are outed by dogs and are saved by dogs. I am totally enthusiastic about this book."

—GINI SIKES, author of *8 Ball Chicks*

"The happy devotion of a dog is the closest thing we have to ideal love. The stories in *Paws and Reflect* remind us of that, and as long as we have dogs, anyone's life can be warmly enhanced. These tales of connection are universal, and along with the provocative facts about dogs that introduce each one, this book offers a warm and satisfying read for dog-lovers everywhere."

—KATHERINE RAMSLAND,
author of *Bliss: Writing to Find Your True Self*

PAWS

AND

REFLECT

PAWS
AND
REFLECT

EXPLORING THE BOND
BETWEEN GAY MEN
AND THEIR DOGS

NEIL PLAKCY & SHARON SAKSON

Manufactured in THE UNITED STATES OF AMERICA.

Published by:
ALYSON BOOKS
P.O. BOX 1253
OLD CHELSEA STATION
NEW YORK, NEW YORK
10113-1251

Distribution in the United Kingdom by:
TURNAROUND PUBLISHER SERVICES LTD.
UNIT 3, OLYMPIA TRADING ESTATE
COBURG ROAD, WOOD GREE
LONDON N22 6TZ ENGLAND

First Edition: NOVEMBER 2006

06 07 08 09 10 **a** 10 9 8 7 6 5 4 3 2 1

ISBN 1-55583-957-8
ISBN-13 978-1-55583-957-4

Book Design by: VICTOR MINGOVITS

NEIL: To my parents, who bought me my first dog, and to Marc, with whom I hope to share all the rest of my dogs

SHARON: To the dogs and the men in the book, and the dogs and the men in our lives, first among them, Richard Fumosa and Jeff Theis

CONTENTS

CONTENTS

INTRODUCTION

Many thousands of years ago, small wolves pulled up beside the campfires of a newly emerged species, man, and forged a friendship.

Instead of disappearing back into the forest, these canines offered themselves as shepherds, guardians, hunters, and haulers. As time went on, they took on an even broader range of duties, as comforters, rescuers, and friends. Dogs have migrated from the primal fireside right into the hearts of our homes.

The truth is that for many of us, our dogs are our children. We don't have to straighten their teeth or send them to college, but we love them, feed them, groom them, sometimes even dress them up, just as if they were little boys and girls. For most dog owners, our dogs are not possessions but family.

Gay men in particular have found joy in bringing dogs into their nuclear circles. Maybe because it's difficult for gay men to create a family that includes human children, their bonds with their dogs are extremely strong. Gay dog-owning couples are notoriously devoted to spoiling their surrogate kids with love and attention. Single gay men are increasingly living the lives of single parents, struggling to combine work, social life, and dog care. Many gay men, single or coupled, seem to have a gift for the special details of dog parenting.

In return, their dogs love them unconditionally, without judgment or regard to sexual orientation; comfort them when they are in pain; and because most men outlive them, teach them extraordinary lessons in how to cope with loss. One thing that every story we've heard has in common is that the dogs involved eventually found a way of enriching their owners' lives.

Because they're always younger than their owners, dogs are like an eternal fountain of youth. Dogs charm us with their puppyish enthusiasm, and gracefully accept the inconveniences of their elder years. Some men tolerate wild excesses of their dogs' craziness and bad behavior. Maybe it reminds them of their own.

For *Paws and Reflect* we sought to craft a sample of the twenty-five stories shared with us by thousands of gay men that illuminate this special and powerful bond. Touching, powerful and often humorous, this collection is representative of a shared, deeply felt devotion. Some stories were built from in-depth interviews. Some were contributed by writers, whom we invited to participate in this project. Three-time Pulitzer Prize–winning playwright Edward Albee shares a poignant story that is the continuation of a conversation of twenty years, since Sharon Sakson first interviewed him about his Irish Wolfhounds for *Sighthound Review*. Actor-playwright Charles Busch reveals in an interview his story of the guardian shepherd who saw him through the bleak aftermath of his mother's death.

Environmentalist David Mizejewski, of the National Wildlife Federation's Backyard Wildlife Habitat program and Animal Planet fame, shares the adjustments he has made to his own emotional and physical habitat to accommodate the well-being of his beloved dogs. Celebrity hairstylist Jack Morton speaks eloquently of lessons he has learned from his dogs about love and humanly elusive compatibility. Several men with *AIDS* write with admiration of the dogs who have been an important part of their therapy. In all, twenty-five gay men from many walks of life and a wide variety of situations illuminate life-altering insights they have gained from the special dogs in their lives.

In addition to being their sweet, cranky, funny, sleepy, unique selves, dogs also represent a way for gay men to connect to other people. A common interest in dogs brought some couples together. It has been a factor in why some break apart. If a man cares about his dog, it is a mark that he may also possess certain behaviors essential to a relationship: the ability to give and receive love, the capacity to tend to the needs of another, the openness to accept the presence of someone else.

Some of the dogs recounted in these pages are already far down memory lane. Some are very much in the present. *Paws and Reflect* is a celebration of the unique bond between any one of us and our canine friends, a celebration of all the dogs we have loved in the past, the dogs we love now, and the dogs of our future, who are only waiting for the right moment for us to invite them to join in our lives.

DOGS OF OUR CHILDHOOD

THE GUARDIAN SHEPHERD

It be wonderful if every child on earth could experience a happy childhood, free from trouble and pain. But in reality that's not possible.

Charles Busch's childhood was interrupted at age seven by the death of his mother. While his sisters and aunts formed a loving, wacky matriarchal society around him, he found a deep well of comfort and strength from a canine source—a giant white German Shepherd named Wolfie.

Wolfie, of course, couldn't have known that his small charge would one day become an acclaimed Broadway playwright and actor. He only knew that Charles Busch needed him, and his job was to provide steadfast company for a damaged child. He did that job so well that forty years later, Charles's voice catches in his throat as he tells me about the giant dog that made his seven-year-old life possible.

Although Charles deeply regrets that he is too busy to have a dog right now, I discovered that in his Manhattan apartment sit two massive, antique, porcelain Chinese Foo dogs that he bought years ago in Hong Kong. They are highly stylized works of art. But it's hard not to notice that once again he has a huge, monster-dog presence in his home, looking over him.

. . . .

WHEN MY MOTHER was alive, we had a black Miniature Poodle named Nicky. He was always driving my mother crazy, jumping up on furniture and on us, but she forgave him because he adored her.

My mother died of a heart attack when I was seven. She was forty-one. No warning. One minute, I had this wonderful, loving mother. The next, she was gone. It was devastating. It was the defining event of my childhood.

The day my mother died, Nicky went right outdoors and ran for miles. He took off. We looked everywhere for him, but we could never find him. It was hard because here we had lost my mother, and losing her dog was like losing another little part of her.

We had no thought of getting another dog. But one night my father came home from work with this little, white, fluffy ball of fur, a German Shepherd puppy. It was a big surprise for the family.

My father didn't have any particular feelings for dogs. He was a perpetual sixteen-year-old. The death of my mother meant that he had to maintain some semblance of family life for us, and he wasn't very good at it. He was a fun and adorable guy. All the ladies he ran around with thought so. He owned a record store in Yonkers, and probably one of his customers brought in this puppy.

But it was a good thing, because we were all sad about losing Nicky and thrilled with this new puppy. Here was this happy bundle of energy, kissing and licking us and romping around. We named him Wolfie.

I took to him immediately. He became my best friend who never moped around, was always glad to see me, never hassled me about homework. We really bonded.

They grow so quickly! In a year this tiny, fluffy puppy was an enormous, long-haired white shepherd. He knew each person in the family—my two older sisters, my mother's two older sisters, my dad—and he had us all figured out. He loved all of us, but he made me feel special.

As a child, I felt alone, and different, at least partly because I didn't have a mother. Wolfie was my friend. He was the one who was with me the most, and all that other stuff didn't matter to him. He just loved me. He was there for me for whatever I needed.

Walking down the street with Wolfie was an experience. He looked like an animal from a fantasy. With his big white body and his enormous head, you could imagine he was a unicorn. When I walked him, cars would stop and people would roll down their windows and stare at us. Here was this thin, sad little boy with this longhaired, white creature. Wolfie knew they were watching, and he was proud. He carried his head high. He had great elegance.

He was so attached to me that he wouldn't let anybody get near me. He'd bark and even bite people. It was a real problem. I didn't have too many friends anyway, but one day, somebody from the neighborhood came a little too close to me as I was walking home from school, so Wolfie bit him. It was a horrible scene. Wolfie and I ran home, and later, after my father got home, the police came.

My father brought the policeman into the living room, where Wolfie and I were lying on the floor in front of the television. I had my arms around him, and he was just lying there, looking peaceful.

"Look at that dog," my father said. "He can't possibly be the dog you got the complaint about. He's not at all aggressive."

"We should still take him in," the policeman said. "He could be a danger in the neighborhood."

I was lying there, just holding on to Wolfie.

I didn't know what I'd do if the police took him away. My father talked to the policeman and showed him how gentle Wolfie was, and eventually convinced him not to take Wolfie. It was interesting that he had these aggressive qualities toward strangers but he was absolutely gentle with me. I could play lion tamer and put my head in his mouth, and he would just wait. He would never think of harming me.

We had a black housekeeper named Beulah Baker who had come from down South, where she had been a pickle picker on a pickle farm. She never did do much housework, but she was wonderful. She sounded a little like Butterfly McQueen. She was very darling and so affectionate to me. We spent so much time in the house together, just Beulah Baker, Wolfie, and me. Beulah used to teach me how to set her wigs, and I was pretty good at it.

On a typical afternoon, Wolfie would be lying there on the floor, and Beulah Baker and I would be busy with combs and pins, working on one of her wigs.

Later we would watch television. I loved old movies—I still do—and I just absorbed the tragic heroines. I tend to watch the same ones that I loved as a child over and over: *Marie Antoinette* with Norma Shearer, *Waterloo Bridge* with Vivien Leigh, *I Could Go On Singing* with Judy Garland, *The Hard Way* with Ida Lupino, *Random Harvest* with Greer Garson, *I'm No Angel* with Mae West, and a zillion others.

Then, my favorite part of the day, my turn to perform. I would mimic back for Beulah and Wolfie these larger-than-life romantic actresses in their classic roles. The afternoon would end with Beulah sitting on the sofa with this huge white German Shepherd at her feet. And I'd be singing Judy Garland songs to her.

Wolfie would sit there staring at me, very alert. He made it seem like watching this skinny little boy singing "The Man That Got Away" was something a dog was really meant to do. That was a typical afternoon in our house.

You can see why not much housework got done. When I was seven, as a special treat, my father took me to the old Metropolitan Opera House to see Joan Sutherland in *La Sonnambula*. I was amazed—it's the story of a young girl who goes walking in her sleep, and sitting there in the audience, I was watching this magnificent redheaded lady drifting through a glorious nineteenth-century painted landscape. When I got up in front of Wolfie and Beulah, I was trying to recreate that for them, the beauty and the dreamy quality. In a way, you could say that my entire career has been an attempt to recreate that first impression. People ask me when I write a play today, do I do any research? Well, I've been researching all my life.

My father remarried. His new wife had children, and the idea of moving in with a bunch of children I didn't know was horrific to me. My father knew that. He made the offer, in the spirit of being caring and fatherly, but he knew I wasn't going to take it. He knew I couldn't live with him in that family, and he didn't blame me.

So I continued living with Aunt Belle, my sister Meg, Beulah Baker, and Wolfie. My older sister was in college. They were my audience. I couldn't be in a school play because I couldn't remember a line of dialogue. I started hyperventilating the moment I hit the stage. It was because I loved it too much. Being "up there" onstage was my most magical dream. I was desperate to be a child star, only no one in my family was willing to exploit me.

Then, when I was around twelve, Wolfie got sick. He started to have epileptic fits, where his whole body would shake, and he'd fall down and jerk and twist on the floor. It was awful to see. I felt horribly guilty. We were so close, I thought something I had done had made him sick.

At first there were long stretches in between seizures, but then he started to get them more often. He was really suffering. I could see that we had to put him to sleep. It was so painful for me, but I didn't want Wolfie to suffer. With Wolfie gone, I was inconsolable. I was so alone.

We got a new dog. This one was a normal German Shepherd, normal size, normal black-and-tan color, not a huge, white giant like Wolfie. We called him Hans. He liked everybody in the family, but he was really Aunt Belle's dog. He liked me, but he didn't think I was the most special child on earth, the way Wolfie had.

By this time I had really gotten lost in a fantasy world. For years I had been just watching old movies and performing for Beulah Baker and Wolfie in the living room. I was flunking out of school. And I was about to go into ninth grade. That's when my Aunt Lillian, who lived in New York City, swooped in and decided I should come live with her.

I've played Auntie Mame three times, and when I do it, I'm just channeling Aunt Lillian. She encouraged me to be everything I was meant to be.

I flourished with Aunt Lillian. She was an amazing lady. One hour with her would exhaust Leonardo da Vinci. She was helpless about some things and unstoppable about others. For instance, she would get lost every time she left the house, even in her own neighborhood. But she could fix a broken radio or make a matador's costume, and she was a woman who could get the president of Condé Nast on the phone if she decided she needed to speak to him about what happened to her November issue of *Vanity Fair*. Moving in with her was the best thing that could have happened to me. But it was the end of my connection with dogs.

Hansie stayed in Westchester with Aunt Belle and my sister. It was kind of odd, how our nuclear family kept switching around. Aunt Belle kept house for my sister for another few years. When my sister was out of college, Aunt Belle moved to New York City and took Hansie with her. Hansie lived out his days with Aunt Belle. He had a wonderful life.

The protagonists of all of my plays are the women I grew up with in that matriarchal household. When I wrote *The Tale of the Allergist's Wife*, people were asking me how I could write such great dialogue for the female characters. They are women who struggle to find a place in the world, and create a new persona for themselves.

I don't have a dog right now. I wish I did. But I think I'd feel horribly guilty every time I left the apartment. My partner and I don't live together, for all kinds of reasons. We each have busy lives and need privacy. You could go into Eric's place any time of the day and think you're in *House Beautiful* magazine. My style is messy. My place is a cross between Sarah Bernhardt's boudoir and a 1960s steak house.

We live down the street from each other. It works for us. But there's not that constant company that dogs need.

The dog I'm most in touch with now is my therapist's dog. Shortly after I started therapy, my therapist rescued an adorable part German Shepard, part Collie. His name's Clarence. I went in for my appointment, and the dog was right there in the room. During therapy, at one point I started to cry. The dog came right over and put his head on my knee and leaned against me. He looked up at me in that way dogs have of letting you know they want to help you.

A friend of mine leaves his cat with me on weekends. I'm not a cat person, not at all. But I didn't expect this cat not to like me. He ignored me. I was doing everything I could to establish a bond with him. And he would look right through me. I felt very rejected by this cat. He made me feel like I was Joan Crawford, the awful stepmother.

Finally I started making his food a little more artistic—not just putting it down on the plate, but taking some time to arrange it. He liked that. He started to take an interest in me and the whole project. I didn't know cats were like that. The whole thing confirmed for me that I really am a dog man. A dog is available for you to hug and love. Cats are kind of sneaky.

Wolfie came into my life at a time when I was completely vulnerable. And that made me bond so intensely with him. He was enormous, he was mystical, he was white. He was the constant, strong, loving, lovable dog that took care of me. It was like he came from an enchanted land. He made me feel that I belonged to somebody.

· JONATHAN CAOUETTE ·

THE TRIUMPH OF *TARNATION*

One of the nicest things that dogs provide for us is the blissful relief of their company. They make few demands and issue no ultimatums. Dogs let us relax.

They let us be ourselves. When your dog is with you, there is someone on your side. In the presence of your dog, you have his attention, affection, and devotion.

As a boy in a family roiling with mental illness, Jonathan Caouette desperately needed all those things. Jonathan is the groundbreaking filmmaker whose documentary, *Tarnation*, tore through critics' assumptions of what documentaries could be. It was selected to be shown at the Sundance,

Cannes, New York, and Toronto film festivals. It was awarded Best Documentary of 2003 by the National Society of Film Critics. It was nominated for an Independent Spirit Award. Roger Ebert called *Tarnation* "a triumph. A film of remarkable power." The *New York Times*' reviewer wrote, "Nobody has ever made a film like it."

The life Jonathan showed on film was ragged and raw and painful to watch. He had started filming his family from the time he was eleven years old, first on Super 8, then Betamax, VHS, Hi-8, and mini-DV for the next twenty years. He added movie clips, pop songs, and scenes from television shows he watched as a child. He created a soundtrack from songs that he loved. He edited the whole thing at home on an iMac, with the structure of the film taking on elements of his own mental illness, which he calls a "depersonalization disorder." The result is a combination of feverish diary for himself and love letter to his mother, whose crazy parents put her through years of electroshock therapy.

It is the ultimate reality program, giving the viewer a "fly on the wall" perspective of an unstable life. So many terrible things happened during his childhood that I was relieved to know that there were sometimes pet dogs for him to play with.

Are dogs helpful to people with mental illness? There is now significant research showing that they are. Service dogs are being trained to help people who become disabled by panic disorder, posttraumatic stress syndrome, or depression, and conditions attributed to brain-chemistry malfunction. They are taught to bring medication, alert someone that help is needed, and nudge their human during an attack of disassociation.

But it's interesting that much of the healing work of dogs is based simply on their presence. The dog's job is to stay near the patient and steady him if he's dizzy, provide stability during a panic attack, nuzzle him if he loses touch with reality. Dogs are able to help mentally ill people by doing what they are best at: being there. Jonathan Caouette made that discovery with his dogs. If only he could have held onto them.

Two dogs appear, briefly, in the film. His current dog, Shiny, wanders in the background of the opening scenes, hovering close to Caouette, who is anxiously waiting to hear if his mother will survive an overdose of lithium. Shiny's son, Miel, plays with a stick in the snow. There have been other dogs in Jonathan's life, as I learned when I spoke to him between his trips to Mexico, where he was screening his film.

. . . .

I'VE LOVED DOGS since I was about four years old.

In general, my memories are tied to two things. A lot are tied to what music was on when a certain thing happened. I think a lot of people associate like that. But also, when a memory comes to me, I'll remember the dog I had then. They were always a poignant part of my life.

My first dog had two names, Sport and Christy. What name we called her depended on what kind of mood we were in. Sometimes she was Sport; sometimes she was Christy. She had come around during a time when there was a lot of tragedy going on in the family. The family circumstances were very bizarre.

My Mom had gotten very sick and had to go into the hospital. She suffers from severe bipolar disorder.

Just before that happened, my mom got this dog from one of the neighbors. She was some kind of terrier, a dirty-golden color. I don't know if she was a purebred or not, but she was a beautiful dog. I have this great picture of her with me when I was about four years old. She's sitting with me, and I have my arm around her. I never wanted to go anywhere without her.

There was a lot of drama in our house. That's what happens when you have someone who's bipolar and schizoid. On those occasions, I would retreat into our backyard to my Slip 'n' Slide or swimming pool. We had this really great overgrown fig tree. I would hide in the fig tree with Christy and pull the branches over us.

I would sit alone with Sport and try to communicate with her psychically. I was trying to see if I could read her thoughts. I still do that every once in a while. You know, dogs are so hypersensitive to whistles and sounds. What would be so strange if they could actually, if not read your thoughts, read your body language? Even if it's just a subtle look in your eyes or a changing of your face?

I would be sitting and Sport/Christy would come up and look at me as if she was trying to tell me something. Or warn me about something, maybe. She would look me in the eye and I would get the sense of a thought, and I would sit still and try to understand what she wanted to say... and then someone would call me. Or I'd hear my mother screaming. Or my grandparents would come over to me. And the moment would be broken. I never got the message.

My grandfather and grandmother were raising me. My grandmother had a hysterectomy and took a long time to recover. My grandfather had to work to pay the bills, so there was nobody available to take care of me. Children's Protective Services got word of that and yanked me out of the home. I had to go into the foster-home system.

When I remember Sport/Christy, it seems to me that she represented the last vestige of normal family life. I was four, almost five. When the foster home happened, I never saw Sport/Christy again. It was devastating. I'll always remember her. She was an amazing animal. After her, stuffed animals had to take over for a while.

I was in the foster-home system for two years. It was a very brutal time. I was beaten and starved, and went through a lot of abuse. There were no dogs in my life during those two years. Finally, my grandparents got legal custody of me when I was seven.

What I really wanted then was to have a normal family. And to me a normal family would include a dog. I would have these conversations with my grandmother and tell her I was getting a dog. There was never a "yea or nay" response. I was one of those people who would stop along the side of a street when I saw an animal, and whether it had a tag on or not, I would kidnap it. Now I know that was a horrible thing to do. But I was so desperate for a dog's company. There were a couple instances where I grabbed a tagged dog that probably belonged to someone in the neighborhood, took it home with me, and fed it for a couple days. Sometimes the dog lasted a week. Sometimes it lasted a month. But my grandmother would call the pound to come pick up the dog, and I would come home, and the dog would be gone. I hope my grandparents didn't call the pound on any of those tagged dogs. Hopefully they just opened the door and let it find its way home.

If I ever asked my grandmother what happened to a dog, she would always pass it off as "He (or she) just disappeared. I just came in the house and the dog wasn't there."

I was careful with these dogs. I fed them, and walked them, and slept in bed with them, and when I left for school, I always made sure the dog was locked up safe in my bedroom. There was no way the dog would have gotten out on its own. Every day when I left for school, I would pray and hope that the dog would be home when I got back.

I went through many dogs that way. Probably ten during my childhood years. I got a Chow, around the time that I accidentally knocked three of my teeth out roller-skating in the swimming pool around the corner from my house. That Chow lasted about a week. A mutt or two or three thrown in the mix. I got a precious little poodle when I was nineteen that was in the house for about a week and a half.

When I was ten, I had a dog named Boomer, after the TV show, *Here's Boomer*, about this cute little stray that traveled the country helping people with their problems. My Boomer was amazing. He would follow me everywhere. We met when I walked to our local park in the suburb of Houston where I grew up, and he followed me home. After that, he followed me everywhere. There was never a need for a leash.

It was very European of us. I love how, in Europe and Mexico and all these other places that I've been, these dogs can be so cool about walking in these big, urban areas with all these buses and cars and pedestrians going by, and they're right by their master.

What I really wanted, during those formative years, was to experience having a puppy, raising it and keeping it for a long period of time. But I never got that, because of my crazy grandmother. On many levels, the animals seemed saner than what was going on in my house. It was the stability factor that I got just by being with a dog in one room, the two of us, hugging each other in our own little world where there was no crazy family and no troubles.

I got so much affection from those dogs. I always let the dog lick me without making a face. I loved to let the dogs lick me on my cheeks, on my nose, on my lips, everywhere. They slept on my bed (and they still do now).

After the poodle at nineteen, I wised up. I left my grandparents' home when I was twenty-three, and there were no animals until I was twenty-four, living in New York City, with my own place. That was the first time that I got to have my own dog and have it stay with me.

My partner, David, initiated us getting what we thought for a long time was an Argentine Dogo by the name of Shiny. We've since learned that she's a mix of something, maybe half pit bull and half Dogo.

David is from Colombia. One day he got a frantic phone call from a friend of a friend from Bogotá. They were living in an apartment in New York temporarily, and had all of these puppies with them. Shiny had been born in Colombia and then flown to Miami and then flown to New York. This poor dog must have been so traumatized just by the air travel! Shiny was about six months old. It was the summer of '97.

All those puppies were beautiful, but Shiny made the most

eye contact. And she seemed like the scapegoat. I think David and I empathized with that. There was something very heart-wrenching about her, something that made her very special. The other ones seemed really macho. She's white with black freckles all over.

She was the icing on the cake of the relationship between David and me. With her here, it was obvious that what we had was something definitely along the lines of a marriage. It felt very official. That echoes what I was looking for as a kid. We've had Shiny for almost as long as we've been together, almost ten years. So we sort of measure our relationship by how old Shiny is.

In my film, there's a real transition when David and I got this apartment and made a family for ourselves. We lived in this wonderful railroad apartment in Williamsburg, Brooklyn. Shiny adjusted immediately. The only problem was that she chewed the hell out of everything. We had so much wonderful furniture, and she just destroyed it all. After a while, I was angry and frustrated but had succumbed to a kind of complacency about it. I collected books and CDs, and she destroyed tons of them. I had to let go and let the universe be what it was. She's trained at this point, to a certain extent. She's out of her chewing stage.

In my early twenties, I was working in a hair salon in SoHo as a receptionist and occasional shampoo boy during the day. Shiney was still a puppy. I walked her around. I think it's cool to see the way people will interact with you if you're walking a dog. I don't think you should get a dog exclusively for this reason, but it's a really cool thing, the way dogs connect people. People say hello to the dog, and want to stop and pet the dog, and they just start talking to you. I enjoyed that.

One day I had to take Shiny to the Humane Society clinic. I hadn't been in New York very long, let alone with a dog, so I didn't know all the rules. At 14th Street, I had to transfer from the N to the R train, so I was standing on the platform when this big walrus of a policeman walked up to me and said, "What's wrong with you? Why do you have this dog here? Is it a Seeing Eye dog?"

I said, "No, I'm just taking her to get her shots."

He said, "Come with me."

We followed him down the platform to an office. I thought maybe he wanted to show her to somebody. He went in the office and came out and handed me this ticket. It was expensive! Three hundred dollars!

I said, "I had no idea it was illegal to take a dog on the subway."

Isn't that terrible? It's ridiculous. We had a muzzle on her and were very careful with her. You would think in a city like New York it wouldn't be a big deal to take your dog on the subway. I was in Mexico City last week, sitting in a cafe where they were serving food, and three stray dogs walked in. They have a lot of homeless dogs there. I don't know if this is a cultural thing, or a Latino thing, but left and right, people were embracing the dogs, petting them, without any fear. I thought, This would never happen in New York.

Just after I got the ticket, I took Shiny on the subway to get home. Just before we got off at our stop in Brooklyn, Shiny peed in the subway car. She'd never, ever done anything like that before. The subway doors opened, and just before we walked off, she peed like mad. It was her way of saying, "Fuck you!" to the system.

Then Shiny had thirteen babies. We kept one of her puppies, and named him Miel, Spanish for "honey." Unfortunately about two and a half years ago, David was walking here in Astoria with Miel very late at night down a one-way street toward a park. A car with a drunk driver zipped around the corner and came down the street, the wrong way, at lightspeed. Miel wanted to protect David. Just as the car came roaring down on them, Miel jumped out in front of the car. The car killed Miel. We came to the conclusion that Miel saved David's life. That was a really sad time for us.

When something like that happens, it changes your whole perception of how amazing these animals are. I don't understand people who won't let dogs on their couch and on their beds. It almost feels like, "Why do you have a dog?" Our dogs are absolutely members of the family. We have a car, and we take them everywhere.

Something has paid off recently from what happened in my childhood. I just recently converged my entire family under one roof. So I'm at the point where I'm taking care of everyone. My mother and my grandfather. We all live in Astoria now, and we have two dogs and three cats. Kind of a full house.

Besides Shiny, our other dog is Lucy. David and I found her by the side of the road in Pasadena, Texas. A guy was selling her for sixty dollars. She's a beautiful terrier mutt. Terriers are kind of a unique subdivision within dogs, and if they're not disciplined, they can be nuts. Lucy sort of looks like Sport/Christy. She reminds me of her, and how close I was to her. And then, the other day, my grandfather out of nowhere told me that the dog was trying to tell him something. He has never said anything like that in his life before. He thought Lucy had something to tell him, but he didn't know what it was. So he's basically saying the same thing that I said about my terrier when I was four. I thought that was really interesting.

But I can't take him back in time and get him to change the way things were. All I can do is try to make things work now, with my family and my dogs.

· MATTHEW PHILLIPS ·

DO DOGS GO TO HEAVEN?

As a child, Matthew Phillips was upset by a Sunday school teacher who told him that there were no dogs in heaven. Though this may have been the thinking once, attitudes are changing. Today, even the most conservative of congregations may offer a blessing of the animals, and people of every religion are coming to accept the spiritual role animals play in our lives.

Buddhists have always regarded animals as beings at different stages of reincarnation. Hindus embrace vegetarianism out of respect for all living creatures. Native American cultures believe that animals have spirits. Attitudes are changing among Jews and Christians; more denominations allow clergy to bless pet weddings and funerals, and the debate over whether animals have souls continues to rage.

An old woman on her deathbed asked James Herriot, the late British veterinarian and author of *All Creatures Great and Small*, if she would see her beloved dog in heaven. He replied, "With all my heart I believe it." He explained his reasoning: "If having a soul means being able to feel love and loyalty and gratitude, then animals are better off than a lot of humans. You've nothing to worry about there."

The poet and novelist Robert Louis Stevenson wrote, "You think dogs will not be in heaven? I tell you, they will be there long before any of us."

American humorist Will Rogers wrote about the dog-and-heaven controversy, "If there are no dogs in heaven, then when I die I want to go where they went."

And the French Catholic monk St. Bernard of Clairvaux wrote in his twelfth-century *Sermo Primus, Qui me amat, amet et canem meum* ("Love me, love my dog"), which seems to put a holy imprimatur on the matter.

Will you see your beloved pet in heaven? A lot depends on what you believe here on earth. For some dog lovers, a heaven without our faithful companions by our sides would be no heaven at all. Matt, who lives with his partner and two Brussels Griffons in New York City, recorded a few of his many memories of his beloved childhood dog, Brandy.

· · · · · · · · · ·

IN THE BACKYARD of our upstate New York home, my father built a tree fort for me in an old and welcoming oak tree. I could climb up six wooden steps and be in my own world. I had a table and two chairs, and various implements that I carried from the house as it occurred to me I would need them: a plate, a fork, two towels, a bottle of instant cleansing and disinfecting hand soap, all my mother's hair combs, her brush, her hand mirror, and, the best prize of all, her scissors.

My English Springer Spaniel, Brandy, stood patiently as I clipped little strands of her bright black and white coat, which gave me a great idea for a career—I would become a hairdresser. With Brandy at their side, my various friends in the neighborhood followed the path out back and climbed up into my tree-fort salon, where they sat down and I went to work. I told each one that their mothers would be so pleased to have their child be the recipient of a free haircut.

Acting like a complete expert, I lifted and cut strands of hair from my friends' heads. One girl had had silky hair that had grown all the way to her waist. All this ended up as clippings on the floor. When I stood back to survey my work, I was proud of the new, short hairdos. I felt myself equal to the famous hairdressers I'd seen on commercials, like Vidal Sassoon and Paul Mitchell.

That evening, the doorbell did not stop ringing, and each time it was another outraged mother, holding her child, claiming I had deformed them. It gave me an idea of what mass hysteria must be like. Unfortunately, I did not like bangs, so I had been particularly careful to lop off any and all hair around my friends' faces. I thought they looked pretty good. But some of these women were using words that would make a whore blush.

Brandy seemed to know that I was in big trouble. She was not allowed inside the house, so she maintained a vigil outside the living room window. She howled each time a parent started in, and she ran to the back of the house every few minutes to look up toward my bedroom to check on me.

My mother made me hide in my room. I was scared when I heard my mother's response to all of these moms. She apologized profusely and reassured them that the minute my father came home I would be severely punished—and with a belt! This appeased the mothers but made me mortally afraid.

Finally my mother came up the stairs. What was she going to do? Was it going to involve belts and spanking and bruises? I kept my mind focused on Brandy. I could hear her outside, barking under my window. That wasn't usual for her. It was as if she wanted me to know she was there and wanted to protect me. The sound of those barks gave me courage.

My mother opened the door to my room and said, "Matthew?"

I decided to be the courageous boy Brandy thought I was. I came out from under the bed. There was something in my mother's hands, and while I was still trembling with fear, she pushed her hands toward me. Through squeezed eyes I saw—a plate of freshly baked butter cookies. The thing my mother baked when I needed to feel better! She ran her hands through my hair and kissed me on the cheek, not just once, but several times. Then she started laughing, louder and then uncontrollably. I started laughing, too. We both laughed till tears ran down our faces. Brandy was still howling outside my window, except this time the howling sounded different. I'm sure of it, Brandy was laughing.

My parents bought a second home at Eagle Lake, about forty-five minutes north of Lake George. We were a Swiss family and our vacations always involved mountains and cold weather, rather than beaches and blazing heat. Our vacation home was a mansion, a seemingly endless maze of rooms, corridors, foyers, and secret passages. For me and Brandy, it was a hide-and-seek paradise.

The estate sprawled across the side of a mountain. It became our family's summer and winter retreat. Each massive room with its solid carved wood door could only be opened by its own key. There were various keys to the many parlors, library, red room, blue room, sewing room, conservatory, and other rooms. Each door to each room was always closed and always locked. Always. It was a real chore keeping all these keys organized, so a skeleton key was attached to Brandy's collar. If we misplaced our own keys, Brandy was always nearby and we could borrow her key to gain access to any of the rooms. Simply by whistling for her, Brandy would come.

The mansion was wrapped by a wooden porch. From here, you could sit and look out over the lake and the Adirondacks Mountains. When I sat on the dock, swinging my feet above the lake's surface, the water was so clear that I could see fish on their daily travels: lake trout, steelhead, walleye, and muskie. Brandy and I spent hours there, my arm hugging across her back, looking out onto the water and the mountains. It was a powerful, majestic view that still stays with me after all these years.

Not long after the haircutting incident, on a hot summer day, my mother packed a picnic lunch for my brother Steve and me. The two of us climbed into our small wooden canoe and paddled off to meet up with our older brother, Rich, and Father on Turtle Island. Brandy was swimming the distance by the side of our canoe. She had webbed feet, a unique characteristic of all Springer Spaniels, and was a powerful swimmer. Her legs cut through the water like oars.

Halfway out into the lake, the canoe started to fill up with water. I became hysterical, not because we were sinking, but because my butter cookies were getting soaked! Brandy was barking and then just disappeared from the water's surface.

Suddenly, a sharp push from under the canoe made us both almost fall out. Brandy was trying to prevent us from sinking, and pushed the canoe up from underneath! She repeated this action again and again, only coming up for air.

Brandy became visibly exhausted when we were still about a quarter of a football field from Turtle Island, but she kept working until we reached the shore. My father and brother were at the shore's edge to greet us. They could see we were having difficulties but didn't realize how serious it was until we got much closer.

My father scooped up Brandy and carried her out of the water. He held her and kissed her face. After that day, he loved that dog as if she was his fourth child. My mother, though, for as long as I could remember, always fervently referred to Brandy as "The Beast," because her thick black and white coat was always covered with matted spurs, thorns and twigs. She was always into something. Brandy was incorrigible. But Brandy was no Beast. To me, she was Beauty. Her big black eyes were like pools, about to overflow. She would allow us to do anything to her, so we did do our best to keep her clean. She was never sick.

That Halloween, I wore the same costume I did year after year. That's the way I liked it. I was a traveling hobo. I wore rags for clothing, lots of patches, a straw hat, and carried a red stuffed bandana on a stick over my shoulder. Brandy always wore her red bandana, too. She joined me on this night like she had done for years, following me door to door.

I had my usual group of five friends, and we planned this particular evening in every detail. This was serious stuff. We carried big pillowcases. We knew the good houses, and the bad houses, the cheap houses, and the rich houses. As we laughed and joked, Brandy would nuzzle our bags for a treat, and we always had an absolute blast. At the end of the evening, knowing I had to unload my pillowcase and give it back to my mother, I started to run toward home. I was right in the middle of the road when Brandy ran at me, full speed, hitting me with such impact that I was thrown backward a great distance. At that exact moment a car came zooming by, missing us both by inches. Brandy lay next to me on the dirt road, licking me and whimpering.

Good girl, I said. Good girl, I'm OK, I'm OK. That car had come barreling out of nowhere on this quiet country road. I hadn't heard it. It had rounded the curve at great speed, totally unexpected. Where I had been, there was nothing left but a shredded pillowcase with scattered treats. My candy had been flattened.

Then it was winter. I remember running through the snow as fast as I could. I was determined to beat my brothers, who were both older, to the lake. I was so anxious to learn ice skating that

I must have fallen a dozen times before I got there. Even Brandy was out of breath. The cold was biting and I could see clouds of her breath, thick and white.

Ignoring the exhaustion from my run, I proceeded to hike down the steep banks of the lake. Before I knew it, I was far from the shoreline and well onto the middle of the lake. My skates were flung over my shoulder.

I remember hearing a loud cracking noise and thinking, What's that? Then the ice underneath me gave way. In the blink of an eye, I plunged into the freezing water. The water was unbearably cold. It filled my mouth, eyes, and ears. I was bobbing up and down, and felt a current pulling me under. I was panicked, and at the same time completely paralyzed. I was unable to scream for help. Breathing was almost impossible.

A strong tug on my jacket hood prevented me from going completely under. Out of the corner of my eye, I could see my dog, sprawled out on her stomach, reaching so carefully to bite the hood of my jacket, pulling me up. She held me for what seemed forever, until my brothers finally arrived and rescued me.

Brandy got a T-bone for dinner that night and for the first time ever was allowed in the house for the evening. My mother said, "Good girl, Brandy," very matter-of-fact. My father just kept shaking his head. He looked at Brandy, then at me, then had to look away. "That dog," he said.

That Sunday, we were all packed and loaded in the station wagon, ready to return home. But where was Brandy? It was starting to snow, and my parents were getting impatient. We spent hours looking for her, but Brandy could not be found. My parents were very concerned and stopped by our neighbors, who lived at the lake year round. The Moshers promised to check for her and leave food on the porch until we returned in two weeks.

My father, the quintessential Marlboro Man in his trademark shearling jacket, seemed nervous. Sensing this made me scared. He repeated out loud, "She's a hunting dog, for Christ's sake, she can take care of herself." It was starting to snow. My great-grandmother, whom we all called Nanny, held me tight so I wouldn't cry, but the thought of losing Brandy shook me to my soul.

Two weeks later, we returned to the house. My father was doing ninety miles an hour. In that speeding car, the entire family was thinking of only one thing: Would Brandy be there? We'd had no news about her.

When we hit the driveway, my father gave an abrupt hoot. There she was, happy and jumping up and down on the porch. A little thin, as she hadn't gotten any dog food from the neighbor. We later learned that Brandy would not allow the neighbor to enter the property, much less approach the porch. She had become very protective of the house and scared the neighbor away because she appeared to be vicious.

Brandy? Vicious? Puh-leeze!

Another scene in my head was from Easter Sunday. My family and I had just returned from church and we were looking forward to enjoying Easter festivities, with all our relatives coming for dinner, a traditional meal with braided Easter bread with eggs baked in, cucumber salad, lamb, and mint jelly (yuck!).

I'd had an upsetting time with my Sunday school teacher that morning. The subject of animals and heaven had come up, and my teacher informed me that only humans enter heaven. He said that's because only humans have souls. Animals do not have souls, and therefore do not enter heaven.

I kept asking, "You mean I won't see Brandy in heaven?" I was on the verge of tears. The thought made me feel physically sick.

This particular teacher made us hold a wooden match between our fingers and recite all the books of the Bible by memory before it burned our fingers. To this day, I can say them all so fast it sounds like a foreign language: genesisexodusleviticusdeutero nomyfirstandsecondsamuelsfirstandsecondkings.

It was an unseasonably mild Easter. I was wearing seersucker shorts with suspenders, a white, short-sleeve, collared shirt, and white knee socks. My mother and I had spent several hours the night before dyeing two-dozen hard-boiled eggs in bright colors, and one of them had come out an amazing shade of pink magenta. I couldn't figure out how I'd gotten that color; it wasn't one of the colors in the kit. It seemed like a jewel to me, one that had appeared by magic, so I laid it carefully on the fake green grass in my Easter basket and carried it with me all day.

I was swinging the basket back and forth by my side, with Brandy tagging after me. I was feeling miserable about this dogs-and-heaven thing.

I decided to visit my playmate Robby to see what he knew about it. Robby lived across the empty cornfields. The fastest way to his house was to cut through the woods. As I followed my usual path, suddenly an extraordinary scent floated to me: the scent of lilacs. Lilacs were my favorite flower. There were clumps of lilac trees that grew in these woods. But this perfumed scent was so strong it was intoxicating. I had to find out where it was coming from. So I took a detour into the woods, to visit my favorite spot, where I knew lilac trees grew in abundance. The scent got stronger as I got closer to them. They always made me smile because they grew in big, crazy clumps of color, with huge bunches of purple, violet, and white. Lilacs are more gorgeous to me than the word "gorgeous" can describe.

Brandy and I wandered among the great oaks, blue spruces, dogwoods, and baby crabapples, across clusters of violets growing sprawled on the ground. Following the rich perfume, we went deeper into the forest, far off the path we knew, where we discovered a field of lilac trees we'd never seen before. In one spot, the sun shot down through the lilacs, creating a perfect circle of light. We sat down. The sun was so warm and soothing that we both quickly fell into a deep sleep. I was curled in a ball, my head resting against Brandy's solid back. My Easter basket lay askew.

We were awakened by an intense light beaming down on us. It grew more intense and I had to cover my eyes. Slowly descending from the sky were two men. Suddenly they were both kneeling at my sides. Brandy watched but didn't make a sound.

They were angels, and they had beautiful white wings.

They were just as I have always envisioned them to be, except they were enormous. I'd guess each one was fifteen feet tall. Everything seemed to be moving in slow motion. The light weakened and I could finally look at them without squinting.

The angels were dressed identically. Both were carrying huge swords in one hand and shields made of gold in the other. What I remember most clearly were the identical robes they wore. They were embroidered tapestry robes, heavily detailed with dog-hunt scenes, embellished with precious stones, diamonds, and rubies. The gold fabric was ornate and heavy. Brandy put her paw on the hem of one angel's robe, and he smiled, put down his sword and caressed her head. No words were spoken.

Through the same opening between the trees came another burst of light. Before me was a figure I recognized immediately from my studies. It was God. He said three words to me: "I love you."

Then He disappeared.

The angels stood up. In the same voice, they told me that God had prepared a special place for all his animals, where I would one day be reunited with Brandy. They told me I could rest assured that all children and all animals go to heaven.

The angels smiled and ascended back through the opening at the top of the lilacs. They were both wearing leather sandals, and that bit of leather was the last thing I saw. Then there was a final gust of wind, and the fragrance of the lilacs grew even more potent, then slowly faded away.

I picked up my Easter basket and ran home. I felt very calm and happy. My mother greeted me and was concerned to see that I was completely sunburned. According to her, I had only been gone for an hour. It seemed to me I had been gone for a long time.

I have never shared this part of my story with anyone before.

Not because I thought that no one would believe me; on the contrary, I'm sure my family would have. I kept the experience to myself because I'm selfish. It was all mine. I have used it to empower myself during difficult times in my life.

Over the next ten years, Brandy, who was literally touched by an angel, saved my life and helped me avoid tragedy on many more occasions. She provided me with love and laughter. She was extraordinary in every sense of the word.

At fourteen, Brandy died in her sleep in upstate New York. I've only seen my father cry twice in his life. Once when we left the hospital room where my mother had undergone major surgery from a ski accident, and that night when Brandy died.

She was wrapped in her favorite blanket and buried underneath the lilac trees. I think of her often and miss her deeply. She was a special dog, a kind of angel, who came into my childhood to love and protect me. Brandy's love felt real and strong back then. Now it's like a place beside the lilac trees I can return to again and again. It sustains me still.

· J.R.G. DeMarco ·

THE LITTLE EMPEROR

Dogs often assume a hallowed place in our memories. The gloss of time burnishes their good qualities and fades their bad ones. But Philadelphia journalist and writer Joe DeMarco remembers the good and the bad in the dog of his childhood, a mixed breed his brother named Caesar. From a pup so tiny he could fit into the palm of Joe's mother's hand, Caesar grew to be a scrappy fighter, always ready to throw himself into battle to protect his family. And that protection lasted long after Caesar himself fought his last battle, leaving behind a lesson about loss that Joe relies on to this day.

Children and dogs have been playmates ever since those first wolves approached the campfires of our ancestors. As parenting becomes more and more prevalent in the gay community, it's important to remember that children and dogs must be trained to live happily and safely with each other. Children should learn the best ways to approach strange dogs and how to treat the dogs in their family. And a hallmark of good training for dogs is that they learn their place in the pack and that their duty is to love and protect the children around them rather than seek to dominate these small humans who may not have the size or personality yet to demonstrate their own dominance.

In the best cases, children and dogs grow up together, as Joe DeMarco and Caesar did, and establish a relationship that nurtures both of them.

· · · · · · · · · ·

CAESAR WAS DEAD. The little emperor who'd stolen all our hearts was gone after eighteen years, and we were left with silence and memories. He wasn't my first dog, but he was the most memorable dog I've ever had the pleasure to call my friend.

His imperial name came from my little brother's overactive imagination. But it fit Caesar's regal personality, which was clear even in the squirming puppy that he was when he entered our lives.

I was fourteen, my sister and brother even younger, and we'd wanted nothing so much as we wanted a dog. A neighbor's beautiful terrier, Sheba, was about to give birth. She had mated with a regal-looking, all-white Fox Terrier. My sister, brother, and I anxiously awaited the results of the match. When it happened, I remember my brother running home with the news that Sheba had produced a litter and that we were to choose one.

We trooped over to the house to take a look at the litter and make a choice. The squirming mass of puppy flesh was too indistinct for me to choose, and neither could my sister or brother. So Mom picked one of the puppies. We were to wait for him to be weaned and then could take him home. The waiting wouldn't be easy, even if we could visit him each day.

A few days later, however, disaster struck—Sheba was killed by a car and the puppies had to be hand fed.

Mom picked him up, a shivering little squealing bundle who barely knew what was going on. He fit in the palm of her hand, tiny, vulnerable, and pitiful. I took one look at him and wondered how we'd keep him alive. But Mom knew more about puppies than I'd imagined. She promptly found a tiny bottle and fed him some kind of milk mixture whenever he wanted.

On the day he came home with us, my brother immediately named him Caesar. I looked at the tiny wriggling pink-and-white pup and laughed, thinking that such a big name would weigh down so small a dog. Watching him move and yawn, blink his eyes and fidget—the sight tugged at my heart and I knew that no matter what his name, I was bound to this little dog.

That was the beginning. The days turned into weeks, and he gained weight and strength and was soon standing on his own and demanding something more than milk. Next came the training—a gentle boot camp. Caesar was a quick learner and took his place among the family members in a short time. I remember staring at him and wondering how that little lump of flesh had become the handsome dog surveying his territory with an imperial air. He was like his father: shapely, sturdy, and smart. Unlike his father, Caesar's white coat was marked with one black furry patch circling his right eye. But rather than appear foolish, Caesar managed to look dashing, black patch and all.

Small and quick, Caesar quickly became the neighborhood favorite. And he lapped it up. He loved the attention but also knew that he had responsibilities and took them seriously. He shook the windows with his barks and with his paws as he pounced on the storm door to frighten passersby. No one escaped his attention, especially not strange dogs, whether or not they had a human companion.

One incident stands out among the rest. It speaks to Caesar's courage as well as his foolishness. But mostly it speaks to the size of his heart and the monumental lengths to which he would go to protect his family and his territory.

A man, not someone known in the neighborhood, decided to walk his Great Dane down our street. Standing outside, I saw him coming and so did everyone else—Caesar, however, was occupied inside at the back of the house. Unfortunately, his business concluded, Caesar made an appearance at the front door just as the stranger and his huge dog were passing our house.

This affront was too much for Caesar. Imagine an interloper of that size having the arrogance to walk through his realm. The Great Dane, placid and stately, had no idea what was about to happen, and neither did any of us. Somehow Caesar managed to push open the storm door. He was small and fast. Snarling and barking, he rushed at the Great Dane and latched onto his back leg.

The tall and courtly visitor was startled and let out a snuffle of surprise. He shuddered and tried shaking Caesar off his leg.

Time stopped. No one could move. Instead we all looked on, jaws agape, eyes wide, waiting for the worst to happen.

Regaining his composure, the Dane turned quickly to see what had clamped onto his leg. There was Caesar, white lightning with teeth, trying to halt the Dane's progress. The Great Dane, with a weary expression, reached back and, opening his large mouth, grabbed Caesar. His jaws wrapped around Caesar's rump, all of it, and Caesar let out a cry of pain.

Several neighbors screamed. I was frozen with horror. I thought this was the end for his majesty and was about to intervene when an amazing thing happened. The Great Dane did not chomp Caesar in two. Instead, once Caesar had let go of the big dog's leg, the Great Dane promptly sat on him until his master directed him to get up.

Caesar, properly chastised and even a little terrified, sprang up and limped into the house. We all rushed in after him, took him into our arms and hugged him. He yelped with a little pain, but apart from a few small scratches due to the Great Dane's teeth, there was nothing wrong. We applied medication to prevent infection, and Caesar took his place in a warm corner of the house to regain his dignity.

Although Caesar had his own concerns (like protecting his treasure horde under my old bed), he never failed in his sensitivity toward family members. He knew just what our emotional state was at any given time and exactly how to approach us. He knew when to lick our faces and when to comfort us by curling up in our laps, warm and solid.

He looked on when, at eighteen, I came out to my mother and the tears flowed. Caesar was there to nuzzle us both, and make us both understand that this difficult moment was nothing compared to the love we shared.

He was also a good judge of character. My late partner was a case in point. Not long after I came out, I brought Bill home to meet my family, and Caesar was at the door to greet us. Without a sniff or a growl, he immediately approved of Bill. And that was what closed the deal for my parents. Caesar didn't like everyone and only some did he take to in that special, this-is-family way. Of course, when Bill discovered just the right place to scratch, he and Caesar were bonded for life. No one had discovered Caesar's S-spot before, so this made Bill special, one of the pack.

Caesar was gone by the time Bill passed away. After more than twenty-five years together, the loss was numbing; grief shadowed my days. If Caesar had been around, he would have mourned with me, licked away my tears, and reminded me of the good times he'd shared with Bill. He would have known just what to do so that I would have felt a little bit better, a little less lonely.

It's those emotional times you remember along with the fun things. The highs and lows of his life mirrored the peaks and valleys of our family's life. Most of all, Caesar was there—always ready to comfort, to guard, to amuse.

Caesar took part in every holiday, every celebration, every illness, every sadness, and every happiness. He never asked much and always gave fully of himself. For eighteen years he was a mainstay and a pillar for us. I don't want to think what eighteen is in dog years. But I'm sure he was immensely old—in body but never in spirit.

His body began to fail him seemingly all at once. At first he couldn't climb stairs, then he needed to be lifted onto our laps, and on it progressed. The White Tornado had begun to slow down. Arthritis forced him to yelp with simple movements and prevented him from acting like the youngster he imagined he was. He would lie in his warm, cozy corner for longer periods, and it was our turn to stay by his side, comfort him, make him happy, and just be with him. It must've been strange for him to feel so earthbound; he was a dog that was more a creature of the air, finding himself everywhere at once as no normal four-legged animal could be—at the door greeting people, running up and down the stairs, in the kitchen begging scraps, always everywhere and anywhere. Eventually he was always in pain and always in his quiet little corner.

It was time, my parents finally told me, to let him go. His pain and suffering were becoming unendurable. Not long before he died, I visited him. He looked tired yet happy to see me. Sad because he could not jump up to greet me, he weakly wagged his tail. So I got down on his level and sat with him. I stroked his fur while talking to him as I had many nights before. I couldn't stop the tears that fell when I whispered my thanks to him for all his love, even when I was a grump or was in one of my deep dark moods. No matter how ugly my frame of mind, he always licked my face or washed away my tears, his tail thumping on the floor. Even at the last, his funny tail thumped the floor, but it beat out a slow, sad cadence.

Caesar realized he couldn't keep up. He wasn't enjoying food or toys or anything; even standing was a painful ordeal. He knew that the time had come to call it quits. And he wanted me to understand.

But no matter what I knew to be true, I couldn't let go. Saying goodbye has never been my strong suit. And I've begun to understand that this was one last gift Caesar was trying to give me; letting go when there is no other choice. Saying goodbye with some dignity for all of us. I've had to say goodbye far too many times to too many people I have loved, and if I'd taken Caesar's final gift, maybe it wouldn't have hurt so much every time.

I took him in my arms that night and felt his weight against my body, solid and sturdy and not apparently ready to give up. But I looked into his eyes and that liquid darkness held all the sad good-bye he could muster. He lay his head against my chest as if to say, "Good-bye, old friend. It's been a good, long run. I just can't do it anymore."

Bill was there that night and realized, too, that we would never see Caesar again. I knew that inside he was all tears and mourning. But in the same way that he faced his own last illness, outwardly he was the soul of strength and steadiness. He let me cry on his shoulder and mourned along with me.

My parents, understanding that neither I nor my siblings could shoulder this task, generously took him to the vet. In their eyes I could clearly see that their hearts were breaking, but they were strong as always.

The next time I visited my parents' home, it was silent—the stillness not shattered by Caesar running to greet me and Bill. A sadness hung in the air. Caesar's reign was over. The house was quiet, his treasure-trove unattended, his kingdom bereft.

Somehow, though, his spirit remained. And if it didn't break the silence in the house, it shattered the silence in my mind. That indomitable, unbowed sense of life, that hunger for action, and that willingness to love—it all came bounding out of some corner in my heart. He had taught me every lesson he had to teach as if he knew the things I'd have to meet as I went down the road without him.

DOGS WHO
MAKE
CONNECTIONS

· Donald Hardy ·

PUPPY WHIPPED

Our dogs often drive us to extremes. Bundled up against below-zero temperatures, we trail along behind them as they do their midwinter business. We carry treats to reward them and plastic bags to pick up after them. We accept slobbery kisses, gassiness, middle-of-the-night barkfests and the occasional chewed-up shoe or cell phone. Why do we do all this?

Scientists discovered that the act of looking at a puppy sends a surge of hormones through the bloodstream that bring about feelings of happiness and a desire to protect. The paternal instinct, usually reserved for one's children, is engaged.

That seems to be why humans have continuously bred dogs to have round heads and big eyes and babylike qualities—the big ones and the small ones, the Cocker Spaniels, Dachshunds, and Schnauzers. Even Rottweilers can put a smile on the face of people who like them. As Benjamin Franklin said long ago, "The more I know of men, the more I like my dog."

Bay Area editor Donald Hardy muses about the deep bonds that "parenting" dogs created for him.

. . . .

THERE HAVE BEEN times in my life when I have felt particularly gay. Way gay. Très gay. Muy gay. Singing with the San Francisco Gay Men's Chorus on the stage of Carnegie Hall gay. Marching in Gay Pride parades gay. Being Vivienne Le Reine, my occasional drag persona—fiercely gay.

But never have I felt as gay as I did the last few weeks of my Cocker Spaniel Casey's life, when I took her for "walks" under the vet's instructions not to let her walk.

The doctor on the case (who was fabulous) was upbeat but slightly evasive about the prognosis. Diagnosis, too, was slightly uncertain, but she did give Casey treatment: a steroid to encourage the marrow of her aging bones to crank out red blood cells; puppy Pepto to calm the stomach so she could take the steroid; antibiotics; and soft food, special stuff that looked, the doctor said, like paté. "She loves it," she said. "She has been chowing down all day. Only feed her this. And no exercise. Out the door to pee, right back in, and rest."

Permanently. She was supposed to do nothing but eat expensive pâté and sleep. It's a dog's life, indeed.

"But Dr. Fab," I said. "I live on a boat, about 200 yards worth of dock from the shore. We have to walk that far for her to get to where she *can* pee."

"No," replied the doc. "That's too far. You carry her."

Silence.

"Well, OK," I said.

I let Casey do her business when I got her home, then carried her down the dock. This wasn't too bad, as she only weighed thirty-five pounds, but I had a strong sense that it would get old fast. I eyed up the dock carts. I'd nearly killed myself the year before when carrying my other dog, Bear, up to the shore for a vet visit. Bear weighed in at eighty pounds.

"Hmmm," I thought. "Maybe I'll get a nice big one that'll fit both dogs, and then *neither* will have to walk . . . assuming they'll let me push 'em. If they don't, that's a wasted 250 bucks. I'll wait."

As I was coming back from walking Bear that evening, Patty and Dennis, my neighbors in the marina, asked what was wrong with Casey. I explained, and they offered a little dock cart they didn't need. About twenty minutes later, Dennis knocked on my deck and said, "Here it is! You'll have to hose it down, but it should work for her."

I climbed up on deck and thanked him, and then looked at the dock cart.

It was small. It was red. It was cute.

I was doomed.

Eleven o'clock rolled around, and it was time for Casey's late night—well, I suppose one ought not to call it a walk—"outing." I took some puppy blankets up and lined the bottom of the cart, then carried Casey up on deck, deposited her in her little cart, and started down the dock.

So. There I was. A forty-seven-year-old, six-foot-two, 200-pound man, pulling a small, fluffy golden dog down the dock in a cute, little red wagon.

Gay.

And the next morning, in daylight, it was worse. People could see me.

I admitted it to myself: I was puppy whipped.

I had lived for eight years on a sailboat in the San Francisco

Bay with my two dogs: Casey, the Cocker in question, and Bear, a giant, aging, increasingly incontinent Schnauzer mutt. If a kid drew a picture of a little house with one door, one window, and a chimney with a pig's tail of smoke coming out of it, Bear was the dog that lived there. Casey, however, was a Cocker from the shallow end of the gene pool. Both were rescue dogs; Bear was completely cheerful and phlegmatic, while Casey was neurotic and high maintenance. But of the two, she was the one who bonded with me, who made me Her Human—and she was My Dog. And now she was sick.

She had always been a bit of a hypochondriac drama queen: Camille with claws. If she bumped her foot on the dock or got a pebble between her pads, she started limping in the most pathetic fashion imaginable, looking at me with huge sad brown eyes, asking why the world was so cruel to her. She would not take a step until I lifted the paw, examined between the pads, and massaged it slightly. I never found anything. Then she'd be off and running as usual, her hips slightly skewed from her front legs, her big ears flopping. But running. She knew a racket. She knew how to work one.

Bear was not a hypochondriac. He had been in a long, slow decline for at least two years. About a year before the incident with Casey, he had a very bad patch and couldn't walk at all. I ought to have put him to sleep but couldn't bring myself to do it; his mind was still there. He still had an appetite. He was still glad to see me when I came home. He regained much of his mobility but his nerves were deteriorating (or so the vet believed), leaving him with less and less control over his back legs and motor functions. By the time Casey was ill, Bear could walk and was cheerful, but I had to pick him up and carry him off the boat.

All of this had happened so gradually that I hadn't really noticed. I'd just adjusted to the situation, equally gradually. When I stepped back and looked at it, I would say to myself, "You are a fucking idiot!" But . . . it crept up. Few pet experiences in my life have been as difficult as that last year with Bear, but every time he staggered over, wagging his tail and rubbing his head between my knees as I squatted down to pet him, I knew why I put up with it: He was happy, even if he was hurting, and every day there were new smells to sniff, and every night new rabbits to chase in dreams.

Bear was the old dog. The sick dog. The dog who would go first. I was ready for it.

And then Casey got sick. She'd been slowing down for several weeks, but since we all were moving slowly because of Bear, I thought little of it. And then she stopped eating. I called the vet, made an appointment, and took her in.

"She's sick," I said and left her there for tests.

I got back in the evening and met with the vet.

"Well," she said, "she's sick."

Duh.

She talked about MRIs and made "chemotherapy" noises, and I looked at her like she was insane. This was a thirteen-year-old dog, in middlin' health. How miserable should I make her? I agreed to a series of tests, noninvasive, but no MRIs, no exploratory surgery. If she had cancer, she had cancer. After a couple of weeks of blood work, a switch to a new doctor, and several hundred bucks, they figured out what was wrong. Apparently she had an immune reaction to her own blood.

And that was when the doctor said, "She doesn't get any exercise. Maybe ever. You carry her."

Feh. Who cares? I didn't really care that I was behaving like a complete lunatic where my dogs were concerned, because, hey, they're my dogs. They depend on me for everything. And they give everything back. So we soldiered on. Or, rather, I did. Morning walks now took close to an hour and a half. The same with dinner walks. And night walks. No matter. Casey still slept curled in the crook of my knees, and Bear snored and twitched in his dreams on the floor beside us.

But of course all things end. Time wins, and even the most loving heart cannot defeat it.

One morning about two weeks later Casey was much worse. She was having trouble breathing, and it was clear she wanted out. So . . . I let her go. I took her to the vet's, placed her on her blanket on the table, and held her head in my hands until she was gone. I'd promised her when I got her that no matter what, I wouldn't leave her alone when she went home.

I kept that promise.

I was wrecked. I didn't know what to do. I'd never been in California without her. She was my girl. And she was gone.

Bear was not. And, as dogs do, he got me through.

For a month he rallied. He was much more affectionate, he tried his best to climb on me every time I knelt to hug him on the dock, he sniffed and snuffed all over the marina when I took him on his slow, painful walks. But eventually he started to slide again. And finally, one Wednesday morning, after he'd lost control all over the boat in the five minutes it took me to wake up, get out of bed, and put on my pants, I reached the breaking point. I called the vet and scheduled a time.

It's hard to make that decision, when, unlike Casey, it isn't clear that he's ready to go. It's hard to make an appointment to let go of a dear friend at a given hour on a given day. But sometimes it's the only thing to do. So six weeks after Casey died, after walking Bear late that last night, lying abed an hour that last morning and watching him sleep, walking him slowly in the morning and afternoon (both times letting him sniff to his heart's content), and stuffing him full of all the soft food and biscuits he wanted, I took him to the vet's. It was a relief, I think, for both of us. The vet approved; she said he'd slid a lot since she had last seen him. And as he lay on the table, his head in my hands, and looked at me, I knew it was right. He was ready to go home, too.

Another promise kept.

And now, for the first time in ten years, I'm dogless. This is OK;

the last two years of their lives, particularly the last two months, had been tough. I looked forward to a rest. The oddest part has been simply waking up and leaving the boat; I've never really done so. But the biggest change was in how I viewed myself. A large part of my self-image was tied up in having dogs. I'm a dog guy, for cryin' out loud. Dogs ran up to me, because I smelled like a big, funny-looking dog.

They don't any more. I'm not a dog guy any more. I'm just a guy.

We have a peculiar life, we single gay men. We have our friends, our families (sometimes), our jobs, and our hobbies. But when, like me, one has been single for a very long time, what we have most is our dogs. They keep us company, make us laugh, console us when we're lonely, and snuggle up against us at night. They're a lot like boyfriends, actually, only nicer. And usually they stick around longer. I know my pups did. And I miss them more than I'll ever miss a boyfriend, new or old.

Someday, when all my dogs are long gone, and I'm old and tired and dim with age or whatever will take me away from this life, I'm hoping there's a little red dock cart to carry me to Rainbow Bridge, where I can laugh and run and roll around again with Casey and Bear and Nudge and Bucket and all of the animals I have loved and will love.

Until then I'll wait for the next dog to come my way. Which she will.

Puppy whipped again, I hope.

· STEVE BERMAN ·

SHI HAPPENS

The love of dogs connects us not only to our canine companions but to other dog lovers as well. I can't walk my Golden Retriever down our suburban street without meeting at least one of his doggie friends—and while they play, I'm making connections to my neighbors and fellow dog lovers. When Steve Berman and Don Hardy became friends, their shared love of dogs helped connect them, and when Steve heard that Don's dogs were ailing, he knew just how Don felt. And though they were separated by the North American continent, Steve had an idea for a present that he thought might help Don cope—a Chinese Foo dog, a souvenir from a trip to the Chinese mainland.

Foo dogs are found in art as early as 200 B.C. and have a strong connection to Buddha. The Foo dog served as a guard, holding a spear in its paw. The mischievous or devilish look on its face helped in its mission at Buddhist temples of scaring away evil spirits. Foo dogs also graced important buildings and palaces until the demise of the Chinese Empire in 1911. As decorative and symbolic elements, they are ubiquitous both in China itself and in Chinatowns around the world.

Foo dogs are often found in pairs, the way Steve Berman eventually found his. The word fu means "happiness" in Chinese, and there is a long tradition of giving Foo dogs as gifts.

Steve Berman didn't know all this when he found a special present for his friend Don. But the spirit of the dog is ancient, mysterious and sacred, and works in ways that only Buddha knows.

. . . .

DOGS GUARD US from many dangers, especially from loneliness. When reading a book, is there anything more reassuring than reaching down from the bed or chair to lightly scratch the fur of your best friend? They create an impression of safety and comfort.

Perhaps that is why in folklore and myth so many guardian beings were based on hounds: Ulysses's dog Argos, the only one who recognized him when he returned from his Odyssey; Cerberus and Garm, who guarded the realms of the dead in Greek and Norse myth, respectively. Some threatened any who crossed their paths, but even the nastiest, the demonic black dogs in Celtic legends, would often show a kind streak, warning innocents of impending misfortune and saving their lives. And in the East there are Foo dogs, which bring to mind a good friend of mine.

Foo dogs, or shi, are the wondrous stone statues found through-out China. Close inspection reveals they actually resemble lions more than any dog. That's because Buddhist tales of lions origi-nally inspired the shi's artisans. There was only one animal in the Middle Kingdom that came close to resembling a lion: the dogs of Foo. Nowadays we call them Pekingese. One myth tells how the breed began as a love affair between a lion and a butterfly (how queer!), and only the Buddha's help allowed them to finally cou-ple. Standing next to these great statues, with their fearsome maws and claws, it's hard to imagine a cute Peke as the source material.

Before my summer 2005 trip to Beijing and Ulan Bator (the capital of Mongolia), my friend Don had to deal with losing his two beloved aging dogs, Bear (a giant Schnauzer mutt) and Casey (a Cocker Spaniel). I kept abreast of their health through reading his blog. He always worried that he would wake up to find one of them had passed during the night. I felt his pain as Casey became sick. At times he wrote so calmly, but there were many entries where I knew his eyes were wet and his insides were shuddering as he typed the words.

I met Don by happenstance at a convention. We're both gay, and sometimes the written word appeals more than a handsome face. He understands parts of my life that my straight friends don't, as if we share a different language. I grew up under the watchful eye of a sweet Kerry Blue Terrier and know how meaningful a dog can be.

Don lives in San Francisco. I'm not far from Philly, too many miles to offer much in the way of comfort. Not that it's ever easy to distract someone who is losing best friends. Don's the epitome of the dilettante with the hounds; I wouldn't be surprised if some psychic discovered that in a past life he wore the red jacket and spurs of an expert fox hunter (though he'd feel guilty about chasing those tails). Then again he's also the sort who likes to roll around on the floor. With his dogs, I imagine, though there have been rumors...

All I could do was offer to bring him back a gift from my trip. I promised him a Foo dog.

After eighteen hours of travel, after the long lines at customs at the Beijing airport, the hotel was a welcome sight. Two pale marble Foo dogs stood guard in the driveway; one silently assured me of a safe stay, while the other had a presence that reminded me of my promise to Don. I petted each dog after asking its permission.

I had no idea that halfway around the globe, Casey's health had deteriorated to the point where Don knew it was best to send her home. He held her head in his hands until she was gone. I think now of how she must have felt. Soft and warm. The marble beneath my fingers had been cool despite the ninety-degree heat.

In one sense, I had no difficulty finding *shi*. Every historical site we visited had them standing proud on pillars and stone blocks. I took pictures not only for myself but for Don. But despite their constant presence, I could not find anything to return with. A Mao watch, even with its snazzy saluting arm as the minute hand, is not much comfort to a dog person (though *mao* translates as "fur").

I looked down many a side-alley bazaar. But enamel masquerading as inexpensive jade or teakwood would have been insufficient. I needed a *shi* that had presence and significance so it would be a better balm.

Don has always laughed at my cynicism, especially my disdain for the mystical or supernatural. I suppose it could be coincidence how the *shi* found me. That would be the easiest explanation. But as I type this, I find myself struck by how purposeful it all seems.

Shortly before I was due to return home, I was leaving an ancient Mongolian Buddhist temple when an old man stopped me on the broken steps. Stooped over and wearing dingy clothes, he was just one of the many peddlers who tried to sell trinkets to tourists. He pulled out a tiny flask for scented oil, weathered coins, a Soviet-era medal. I shook my head at each, and then he held out in creased hands two tiny bronze Foo dogs. I looked down and stopped, which encouraged him to smile at me with twin rows of broken teeth.

I picked one up. It was heavy and warm from being carried in his shirt pocket. Fine details brought back to mind every carved stone shi I had seen on the trip. I looked back over my shoulder at the temple I had just left. A sense of dignity and lost splendor filled me. I felt a blend of melancholy for all that had been lost— for the cultural heritage of that nation, for Don having to bid farewell to his dogs—and yet this sadness was not bitter. I pulled out the paltry sum he requested and then doubled it for the old man and bought both. He seemed surprised at my generosity.

I kept the two bronze shi wrapped and safe in my luggage. They were as precious as the exotic purple jade earrings I splurged on for my mother, more rare and meaningful than the handmade wood demon mask I purchased at the ancient and ruined capital of Karakorum.

My travels were all safe. Even when I climbed down from a mountain shrine and lost my footing on a treacherous trail, I did not plummet down the rock face, only bruised my tailbone. The prediction of safety made by the Foo dogs at the hotel had come true.

I kept my promise to Don as well. Upon my return to the States, one of the first things I did was mail off one of the bronze shi. Don's e-mail of thanks, telling of his surprise and joy at receiving such a gift, remains a treasured thing, and the bytes had the weight of pen and ink on parchment. Yet even with all my best of intentions, a little bronze figurine cannot change fate. Bear passed away the following month. Don, for the first time in so many years, was alone. How quiet his surroundings must have been. No more the gentle wheeze and groans of elderly dogs lulling him to sleep. I wish the little shi could whine just once for him.

What happened to the other bronze Foo dog? I had kept it for myself, a source of comfort and protection. I remember unpacking and unwrapping it, but now it seems missing. Just before I fall asleep, I imagine it somehow patrolling my apartment, looking into the dark recesses, keeping me safe. I often wonder, If I let my hand slip over the side of the bed, my fingers just an inch or so from the floor, would I feel warm metal brush against them?

· LEV RAPHAEL ·

INTO HIS EYES

Prolific novelist and essayist Lev Raphael has the keen ability to peer into the heart of any situation. When we asked for his insights on the canine-human bond, we had no idea how deeply he had already explored this topic, through his relationship with a beloved West Highland White Terrier.

His choice of a Westie is intriguing, as the terrier breeds have a reputation for being independent and stubborn, and a challenge to train. The West Highland White Terrier Club of America says about their breed, "If you want a cuddly lapdog, a Westie may not be the right breed for you." Like so many terriers, Westies are tough, feisty, and, according to the breed standard, "possessed of no small amount of self-esteem."

But Lev Raphael has met many challenges in his life, beginning in a childhood with parents who were Holocaust survivors. His memoirs and his "second-generation" novels explore the ongoing impact of the Holocaust, a tough subject about which he writes movingly, and often humorously, in a way that illuminates the human condition. And here, as he gazes into the eyes of his beloved Westie, he illuminates for us the connection between man and dog, one that is often so deep no words are necessary in order for full communication to occur.

Author Edward Hoagland wrote, "In order to really enjoy a dog, one doesn't merely train him to be semihuman. The point of it is to open oneself to the possibility of becoming part dog." By training his dog to maintain eye contact, Lev Raphael entered into a communication beyond words.

· · · · · · · · · ·

I'M READING IN my study, where books climb up every wall, and Kobi pads in, glancing at me, so I say, "Go ahead," and he jumps onto the comfortable golden velour armchair opposite me. Sometimes it seems less that he's asking for permission and more that he's simply interacting with me the way a human would say hi or touch someone's shoulder in greeting.

Identical to the chair I'm in, it's his favorite chair—in this room, anyway. He has two other favorites. One is a cocoa-colored Scandinavian leather recliner in the living room. The other's a small blue tub chair in the bedroom I share with my partner of seventeen years in a heavily treed mid-Michigan suburb filled with 1950s ranch houses.

If someone's sitting in this particular chair, he'll wait and stare. He can be deferential at such moments, but he's very clear about what he wants. He's a Westie, and as they say, Westies will not be ignored.

He spends so much time on this chair—when he's not out terrorizing squirrels in the large backyard—that we call it "his chair." He likes to snooze with his head off to one side, cushioned by the chair arm.

When my partner and I leave him alone at home, we say, "Kobi, it's time to guard the house," and he heads right to that chair. When we need to de-mat him or do any other grooming and health maintenance like brushing his teeth, we say, "Kobi, it's time for grooming," and he heads for the chair.

He could manage to jump onto it when he was tiny, but he was scared to jump off, and he would pace back and forth and whine. Like a father encouraging his child to dive into a pool, I would pat the thick brown rug and say, "Jump!" and praise him when he did. I'm always remembering what he used to do and used to be because, like any parent, when I look at Kobi, the past is a pentimento, creeping out from what's on the surface. I see him at different ages whenever I look at him, so that each moment is many moments and I enjoy who he was just as much as who he is right now.

Sometimes he sits up in this chair after he has climbed onto it, looking at me, and it's clear he wants something: to be petted or spoken to. I'll stop what I'm doing to comply. Then he lets go, lies down, and disappears into sleep. If he's a bit restless, I give him a hand signal from my chair, my right hand out, palm down, lowering it as I say, "Rest, rest." It's what we did when we were crate-training him as a puppy and he needed to get used to being in his crate at night. Only back then we lay down outside his crate to mimic what we wanted him to do. We were doting, dotty parents.

But it paid off because now it always works. As if he's being hypnotized, his eyes start to flutter shut with each "Rest" and he sinks down into the chair. His chair.

Today, however, he doesn't need coaxing, he needs something else. Though he seems to be settling in for a snooze, his eyes are still wide open. I meet his gaze, hold it, and we stare into each other's eyes as we have ever since he was a six-pound puppy. It goes on for half a minute. It goes on forever.

"I love you," I say quietly, as I did when he first came into our lives, over and over, and slowly his eyelids droop and he falls asleep. In their dog-training books, the Monks of New Skete strongly believe that accustoming your puppy to eye contact from the very beginning will lay a strong foundation for future training, but even more important, it will build a deeper relationship, a "real exchange between animal and man." These are moments as rich with connection as when a parent gazes into the eyes of a suckling infant and a whole world of mutuality opens up between them.

Did Kobi seek this extra level of connection right then when he looked at me from his chair, or did he just accept it? I can't be sure. But as always, I marvel at the way he is entwined around my heart.

I grew up with a pedigreed, medium-sized German Shepherd whom we rescued from a pound at seven months, but he wasn't really my dog; he belonged to my father, adored my father. As the youngest in the family, I was tolerated and played with. I did my share of walking and feeding Rippy, and I played with him and brushed him sometimes, but I wasn't deeply involved in his upbringing or care.

Kobi is the first dog I've raised from a puppy, and I was completely unprepared for the depth of the relationship that we established with each other from the very first weeks, the sense of intimacy.

It started with his physical closeness. When we first adopted him, he was small enough to be held in my hands. He was also small enough to sit on me, even stretch out on me. He quickly made up his mind that sleeping on my chest when I was sprawled on the living room couch was a good thing. He'd clamber up, pad over, plop down, and tuck his chin in as close to mine as possible. As he'd fall asleep, we'd be breathing each other's breath. The scent of his coat enveloped me—a cross between popcorn and cardboard—and I felt a level of peace and contentment I'd never experienced before, as relaxed as if I were meditating. I'd wonder if being surrounded and sheltered by me was for Kobi a return to the litter, analogous to what it felt like to lie against his mother. He could even fall asleep on me if we were playing and I stretched out on the floor on my back. He would climb up, plant his chin between my pecs, and then his eyelids would start fluttering closed.

On the couch, he simply did what he wanted, and because I wanted it, too, that was fine. But just as I learned during potty training him the signs that meant he had to be whisked outside, I also soon learned to pay close attention to everything he did and "said." Our Westie breeder, Janet, would often respond to our questions about dog training by advising us to "ask Kobi," and so we learned how to ask him, and he in turn learned how to tell us.

Like all puppies, he was curious and playful, and within the first month, he initiated a game. One evening while I was chasing him around the house, he dashed into my study and slid under a skirted hassock that hid him completely. I stood there laughing and then said, "Where's Kobi?" He poked his nose out just enough for it to be seen. I laughed even more, and it seemed he was waiting for me to do something. So I reached in and started to wrestle with him, and he play-growled and mouthed my fingers. In a few days the game developed variations. If I didn't ask "Where's Kobi?" quickly enough, he would grunt louder and louder to get my attention. And soon I was reaching in from all sides as he twisted and turned to "get" me.

This game was something we co-created and each can initiate. He's three years old now and weighs twenty-one pounds, but if I say "Where's Kobi?" or "Do you want to go under?" he'll slither under the hassock (it's not as comfortable a fit as it used to be). If I'm at my computer and resisting his blandishments of barking or squeaking a stuffed toy, he'll dive under the hassock because he knows I'm guaranteed to respond. He also created the bedroom version of "Where's Kobi?" by crawling under the covers and scooting around there while play-snarling at us as we tickle him.

I didn't expect that we would be interacting like this, but the communication kept deepening because I kept watching him and studying him, and he learned that he had a responsive audience. The first time he sat down next to his water bowl rather than drinking from it, I knew without looking that he wanted fresh water. Kobi quickly learned the words "fresh water" and started following me to the kitchen sink when I'd ask if that's what he wanted, and I refilled his dish.

He barked when he wanted to go out into the backyard, but the first time he didn't rush through the open door and instead reared back with one front leg up, I was sure he wanted me to come with him (the gesture even looked like an excited "After you!"). I was right, because outside, he started to play "keep away," where he grabs a toy, brandishes it at us and runs off daring us to get it from him. Now if I hesitate at the door when he wants a companion, he'll either push at me or refuse to go out unless I lead the way.

Our bed is too high for him to jump onto, so we keep a hassock from one of the bedroom chairs alongside it as a "ladder." Once I'd forgotten to move it over and found him sitting in the bedroom by the bed. He looked at the hassock, then looked at the bed, then looked at me. I knew what to do.

I'm a writer and work at home, so I look forward to walking him through our subdivision rich with hundred-year-old trees, but sometimes I can get distracted and forget I'm out there for his health and mine, and walk too fast and don't allow Kobi enough sniff time. After all, smelling is the main way he experiences the world. Kobi doesn't just stop when he wants to keep sniffing, he puts a paw down on his leash, and if I still don't get it, he puts two down and glares at me, his head lifted in what looks to me like challenge or annoyance. I listen.

Despite all the dog books I read, Websites I visited, and conversations I had with our breeder and other dog owners, something simple but beautiful was never entirely clear to me. Bringing Kobi into our home was creating a new relationship, one that evolved between us. He has taught me what he wanted, and I have taught him that when he expressed his needs, he would be understood. This has built confidence and trust between us and made Kobi a well-adjusted, balanced dog. And one who seeks out eyes. Another Westie parent down the street often remarks on the way Kobi is studying us, watching us.

And merging with us. As when he climbs onto our bed at night, settles down next to me, then lifts his head up and looks right into my eyes for one last shot of connection before he tucks his head in and disappears into his dream world while I go off to mine.

· A N D Y Z E F F E R ·

DISCOVERING
THE DOG LOVER WITHIN

Are we born loving dogs, or is that something

we learn? Can the right dog convert even the most

ardent cat lover? When journalist Andy Zeffer moved

in with a roommate in Fort Lauderdale to save on rent, he
discovered that the apartment came with a catch: there was
a third roommate, an Eskimo-Chow mix named Colby. Their
relationship, which began with shared interests (walking
and treats), has blossomed, as Zeffer has discovered the dog
lover inside himself.

Loving dogs can have significant health benefits, too. Studies at the University of Missouri–Columbia have shown that just a few minutes of petting your dog can increase the levels of several types of feel-good chemicals in the brain, including serotonin, prolactin, and oxytocin. This supports research in South Africa that demonstrated that fifteen minutes of quietly petting a dog can cause beneficial hormonal changes in both dog and human.

Anatole France, who won the Nobel Prize for Literature in 1921, wrote, "Until you have loved an animal, a part of your soul remains unawakened." Andy Zeffer's passage from being uninvolved with dogs to coming to love one, is a story of that awakening.

· · · · · · · · · ·

I'VE ALWAYS BEEN a cat lover. Growing up I had a cat that I loved like crazy. As a small child my family would pass by a store called Pepee's, which I couldn't quite pronounce right. Hence we named him Pebee. That cat was so cool. I had him from age three to eighteen, and when he passed, my whole family was heartbroken.

You see, my sister and I were not allowed to have a dog: too much responsibility. My parents didn't want to nag my sister and me to take a dog for a walk on freezing winter mornings. Plus, if we wanted to go away for a weekend, a cat was no problem. Just be sure to leave enough food and water, and any feline is more than happy to be the ruler of the castle. As a family, we entirely appreciated the independent streak in cats.

I often found myself defending the attributes of cats to sworn dog lovers, arguing their superiority.

"Cats are standoffish," a dog lover would spit.

"That's not true. They're just independent. In that respect they're more like people. They don't appreciate being pushed around."

"Well, cats are dumb. They can't roll around and fetch a paper."

"They have too much pride and dignity. If you think cats are dumb, you haven't seen my cat the minute the can opener hits the tuna. You haven't witnessed him leap at a doomed rodent."

"Cats aren't affectionate!"

"That's crazy. You should hear my cat purr like a motor when I pick him up. Or see him curl up on my chest when I'm sleeping."

"They're gross. They lick their own butt hole."

"That's because they are capable of cleaning themselves, unlike dogs that start to smell like toilets if you don't throw them in a tub of water after a few weeks."

So the back-and-forth arguments with dog lovers ensued, with surprising frequency and passion.

As a young adult, I have done my fair share of moving around, nixing owning a pet whether it be a cat, fish, or turtle.

My animal-free time span came to end when I moved back to Fort Lauderdale after spending a season in Provincetown. I landed in a studio that looked cute and charming during the day but at night turned into one giant bug trap.

When a colleague of mine was looking for a roommate, it seemed serendipitous. The office was a short drive from his apartment. Our interests and friends were different so we were never in peril of getting on each other's nerves.

His only concern was how I would get along with his dog.

Understand, I have never been a dog hater, though sometimes the tiny yappy ones grate. There is a soft spot in my heart for animals. This might be shameful, but when I hear about bombs going off left and right on the news, I'm calm. But if a report of animal abuse or even a beached whale flashes on the screen, it's too much for me to bear. I consider myself pretty adaptable; however, I was a bit concerned about how well I would tolerate Colby.

Colby is a beautiful dog. Part American Eskimo, part Chow, he has the most gorgeous, fluffy cream coat with orange undertones.

His deep-brown doe-shaped eyes gleam when he looks up at you and boast rows of tiny white lashes. His black nose is truly as cute as a button, and his snout is noble and handsome. When he is happy, his mouth lights up in a smile from ear to floppy ear.

Except that wasn't the expression greeting me on the day I moved in. My roommate is quite the man about town—and not around when it came time to trudge my stuff inside. What I got from Colby was a snarl and a not-so-attractive curl of the lip, which translated to "I have sharp teeth. Watch out."

Adorable as he was, at forty pounds Colby was quite capable of hurting me if he wanted. My first move was straight to the kitchen for a dog biscuit. Thoughts raced through my head of kids I had known in school who bore scars from dog bites, pit-bull attacks on the evening news, even that poor lesbian in San Francisco mauled to death by her evil neighbors' Presa Canarios. (Admittedly, I've always leaned toward the dramatic).

Game for a cookie, Colby stopped his snarling to chow down, but as soon as he swallowed the last crumb, a low growl ensued. My next move was to grab Lynn, the reclusive next-door neighbor who babysat Colby during my roommate's frequent travels.

After a few days Colby became accustomed to me, differentiating my presence from that of an intruder, or the mailman, whom he seems to think is planning something diabolical every time the mailbox clinks.

A former New Yorker, I enjoy walking and miss the simple pleasure of waking up in the morning and making the brisk steps to the Starbucks a few blocks away. Once Colby realized my penchant for taking walks, it was the beginning of a mutual love affair. Going around the pebble track of a nearby park became a shared routine. To my delight, I began to look forward to the dance of appreciation he would make as soon as he saw me open the cabinet drawer and pull out his leash.

It always starts with a jump up, then a series of leaps in a circle, culminating in his running over to me, kneeling down, and raising his head high in the air so I can clasp on his leash as fast as possible. If he is feeling especially exuberant, he will take his end of the leash into his mouth as we're walking out the door, as though he is leading me.

Passersby often stop to compliment Colby and ask questions such as "How old is he?" or "How long have you had him?" The first few times I would explain that he was actually my roommate's. Soon, though, I grew so fond of him that I stopped bothering. After all, for that moment he was mine and in my care.

The feeling of being a proud father overtakes me on these jaunts. Whereas a lot of other dogs are barkers or hysterical growlers trying to bolt away from their leashes with all their might and giving their owners a hell of a time in the process, Colby is like the cool dude. It is like having a chill son who surfs or snowboards. His response is to look at these frenzied fellow canines with a puzzled glance, as if to say "Man, what is your problem?" then calmly keep padding along, going back to what pleases him most, sniffing every object he passes. His legs seem to trot more than anything. If a sight or noise catches his attention, he will freeze with one front paw up in midair, like a show horse competing for a blue ribbon.

The only time he gets out of control is when we near a small bridge that covers one of the canals in our Fort Lauderdale neighborhood. It seems to be a favorite hangout for iguanas, and chances are good that you will see one of the vibrant, lime-colored creatures basking on the cement embankment. Like the man of steel, Colby can spot the critters at a distance impossible for the ordinary human eye. I usually know it when the head springs forward, the eyes widen, the excited panting begins, and I am suddenly being dragged up the slope toward the railing of the tiny bridge. As soon as we get within ten feet of the iguana, the lucky lizard catches on and the next thing heard is a small splash. A few houses down the canal the amphibian will scurry up the canal wall, teasing Colby until I manage to coax him away.

Not only have I found myself walking Colby, but I also bathe him, feed him, even take him for short drives in my car. My roommate is a strict disciplinarian, seldom, if ever, slipping Colby human food. Now he knows who to go to when he wants a chunk of cheddar, a few pieces of chicken, some wedges of tuna. A high-pitched chant of "Treat!" has him running in from the yard when all else fails, fluffy cream fur flying and bushy tail curled up like a crescent.

I'm more of a homebody than my roommate, so I've had my fair share of evenings on the couch. Usually it goes like this: Colby will be lying on the floor, his front paws folded and his back legs splayed out like a frog. Inevitably he will work his way to the couch, prop up his head and front legs on the sofa, his hind feet standing on tiptoe. How can I not start stroking that furry white head, scratching behind those floppy ears, kissing the forehead above those glassy brown teddy-bear eyes? With happy snorts and huffs, he springs into action and does a different kind of happy dance, one in which he fervently rubs the top of his head onto the leather seat cushion, his butt sticking straight up in the air, keeping up with the gleeful, snorting sound effects the whole while.

When I am not up to facing the traffic or in no mood to meet another deadbeat guy at one of Fort Lauderdale's many gay bars, when I come home exasperated and exhausted from my job, this gentle creature eases my woes.

This adorable dog who first snarled at me when I came into his home now comes into my room while I'm sitting at my laptop and flops down beside me, letting out whiny whimpers until I turn away from the keyboard and scratch him.

You are probably wondering what happened to the sworn cat lover I claim to be.

I have been seduced by cuteness, mesmerized by this puffy-coated mass of divinity. When I go away on trips, the one thing I find myself missing is Colby. There is something about having a creature that is always excited and happy to see you. It's nice to always be wanted, needed, and accepted.

The day will come when my roommate and I will part ways, and he will be taking Colby with him. I'm sure I will be tempted to kidnap him, because leaving his side will fill me with melancholy. I am always joking how I would love to take him to be cloned.

Through all this the dog lover in me has been awakened, and I have discovered something within that I had no knowledge existed before. When the day comes that I get my country home, whether it be on the Cape, in the Berkshires, Catskills, Hudson Valley, or wherever, it will be filled with both a dog and a cat.

· JEFFREY RICKER ·

DAKOTA

One of the many fascinating facets of dog owner-

ship is that dogs have an uncanny ability to connect us

with members of our own tribe. Many gay men told us

they had discovered that walking their dog is an easy way to
meet other men. Science backs them up: A study in which
some men walked through a park alone, while others walked
with a dog, proved that people were three times more likely
to stop and talk to the man with the dog. They perceived the
dog owner as friendlier.

Jeffrey Ricker has been on both sides of the "canine bonding"
experience, using his dog first as a way to connect with other

men, then as an excuse to avoid connecting with them.

He and his Newfoundland–Border Collie mix bonded so well that Ricker realized he was content to live on his own, with only his dog for a roommate —but he didn't want the life of a permanently single man. He wanted a partner and forged a connection with a man who was also a dog owner.

He writes about the problems that can come between men who each depend on the company of their dogs as much as on the company of each other.

. . . .

MY RELATIONSHIP WITH my dog almost cost me my relationship with my boyfriend. That would have been a sad irony, since Dakota—that's my dog—is the reason I started dating again.

Dakota's the name the dog came with. When people ask (and they always ask), "North or South?" I reply "Dodge." I drove a pickup truck, a Dodge Dakota, at the time I adopted him, in July 2001, and I didn't see a reason to change his name. I bought the truck because I'd just bought a house, and I'd bought the house because I wanted to get a dog. Dakota's a big dog—a Newfoundland–Border Collie mix, as best as the vet could determine. I got him from the Humane Society, so in the end he only cost me $62,100: $100 for the adoption and shots, and $62,000 for the house—$74,168 if you include the truck, but I didn't quibble.

What amazed me about Dakota was how easy he was. He already knew how to sit, stay, and heel. He was housebroken. He got along with my two cats.

Boyfriends should be so easy, I thought.

When I got Dakota, I was single. All my friends said he would be a total guy-magnet. I could see their point—unlike me, Dakota has never met anyone he didn't like. What he lacks in intelligence, he makes up for in geniality.

He's kind of a blonde like that.

I tried to take Dakota with me running around the neighborhood—I pictured taking him, later, to the park and hitting the running trail, where there's never a lack of hotties and their dogs. He was great for the first couple hundred yards. But Dakota turned out to have this habit of wanting to stop at every tree, signpost, or mailbox and read the scents. Eventually I realized I risked dislocating my shoulder from all the sudden stops, and we compromised with a brisk walk. By the time we walked to the park, though, he was exhausted—not surprising for a dog wearing a full-length black fur coat in the summertime. After that we settled for walking around the block a couple times as our regular walk, and he did turn out to be a magnet for attention—thanks to him I met every little kid and senior citizen on my block. So much for hotties.

I didn't get Dakota in order to attract the hotties, though. I got Dakota because all the hotties never seemed all that interested in me. Maybe my occasionally paralyzing shyness or general cluelessness was to blame for that, but after listening to my friends lament their man problems ad nauseam, I was more inclined to keep my nose in a book and my dog sitting nearby. So I had to vacuum a little more often because of his penchant for shedding—so what? I simply bought a better vacuum cleaner ($86.95 plus tax).

It might seem odd, then, that Dakota was the reason I started dating again. Before I got him it had been at least a year since I'd gone out with anyone, and another six months before I gave men another shot. Why did I dive in, when I was perfectly happy staying out of the dating pool and spending time with my dog?

Because I was perfectly happy staying out of the dating pool and spending time with my dog.

I asked Susan, my friend and fellow dog owner, "What if I've tried to trade in Mr. Man for Mr. Mutt?" Susan, who was married with a baby on the way, didn't think it was such an unreasonable trade-off.

"You've given Dakota a second chance at life, and in return he gives you all the love and companionship that a man would," she said. "Well, almost all. And what he can't give you that a man could, you can take care of yourself."

"But what if I'm using Dakota as an excuse to avoid men?" I countered.

"Are you?"

And that's why I started dating again.

At first, I thought Dakota would be a good screening device for men—if he didn't like them, then it was probably a safe bet that I wouldn't, either. This strategy collapsed when it became apparent that he was no judge of character. Dakota rolled over on his back to have his belly rubbed by every man who walked through the front door.

My dog, it seemed, was a tramp.

If he wasn't such a good judge of character, Dakota's personal habits were excellent at weeding out the too persnickety. Dakota's a jowly dog, and it takes no effort on his part to swipe a band of drool across the leg of someone's pressed trousers. Then there's the aforementioned shedding, which pretty much guarantees that anyone walking into the house will be carrying a little bit of him out when they leave.

This turned out to be a problem for very few people, and more than a few times I think they liked Dakota better than they liked me. There was the redhead with two dogs of his own who took to Dakota quite well; unfortunately, he also had such social phobias that he never wanted to go out anywhere, and my desire to do things that involved leaving the house proved too much of a hurdle for him. There was the Cuban from New York City who didn't meet Dakota until after our short-lived, disastrous initial encounter. While there was no love lost between the two of us, I had to keep my eye on him lest he try to spirit away my dog. Then there was the Syrian doctor who was generally against dogs because of cultural reasons; Dakota managed to win him over, though, even when I couldn't.

By this point, hanging out with Dakota and a book seemed like the sanest option.

They say you take on the traits of the pets you bring into your home, but I don't think I became any more lovable or genial under his influence. I had hoped otherwise; I've always been a bit too bristly, a little too ready to shoot off my mouth. If any dog is the exact opposite of that, it's Dakota. By all rights, I should probably own one of those little yappy dogs or a pit bull.

As it turned out, the guy I did finally end up with, Mike, owns one of those little yappy dogs. Bonnie's a lovable miniature Dachshund with seemingly limitless energy. She is also deaf as a post, high-strung, and occasionally snappish, especially after she wakes up. To Mike, Dakota seemed like a cakewalk in comparison.

Dakota, though, is a big dog, and big dogs make big messes. And that's where he has had at least one affect on me: He has made me much less slavish about keeping a scrupulously clean house. At my old house, I only vacuumed when little tufts of his fur rolled across the floor like tumbleweeds. The corners of doorways were smudged gray where he'd rubbed against them. The kitchen floor was best not discussed except to note that dog drool has remarkable adhesive powers.

Mike was well aware of this, having spent a lot of time at my house during the first year we dated while his new home was being built. But it's one thing to tolerate a dog's mess when the house in question isn't yours, which he discovered when I sold my house and moved in with him in October 2005.

It's still another thing when your dog starts exhibiting behavior that could get him sent back to the pound.

I honestly didn't know what to think when Dakota started acting out. Suddenly my perfectly behaved dog was peeing on anything in the house that was new to him. Whenever we turned our backs, he went down to the basement to find a new box to mark. He also took to eating the cats' food, which explained his fishy breath.

One evening before we went to bed, we decided to put him in the laundry room for the night to at least keep him from peeing on the carpet. It was an unnerving surprise the next morning to find him standing at the foot of the staircase when we came down—and to find the laundry room door gouged up, wide open, and some well-chewed dirty laundry scattered across the floor.

I thought I was a terrible parent. This was like that mother you see in a grocery store with the child who's screaming out of control, clutching the candy rack and refusing to let go. And I figured Mike was thinking the same thing, because after the laundry room incident, each conversation was tense with all the things we weren't saying to each other: Why couldn't I control my dog? Why couldn't he lighten up?

Dogs being the intuitive creatures they are, Dakota picked up on all this. I didn't know dogs could frown until Dakota started slinking around with a long face, his head down. My child was miserable, and it was all my fault. I had taken him away from the only stable home he'd likely ever known, and he was letting me know that he didn't like it.

My friend Ryan said that our blended household reminded him of The Brady Bunch, only with pets instead of kids. If that's the case, then Dakota was my Jan. I guess that made me Carol, and I wondered what Mrs. Brady would have done if she were forced to choose between her new husband and her troubled child. My vet said Dakota needed time to acclimate to the new house. "He's just trying to get it to smell like him," she explained. "Once he's made his mark on it, he should settle down."

My dog, it seemed, was a drama queen. I have no idea where he could have picked up *that* trait.

The vet was right, though: After a couple of months, Dakota no longer seemed plagued by abandonment issues. He just needed time to understand that this new house was as much of a home as our old house, and I had to get used to the idea that my dog was not the perfect companion I had always believed him to be. Like anything else that's worth doing, taking care of and training a dog can be hard work, and I had been spoiled up until then.

I hadn't been very patient, either, but then I hadn't needed to be patient with Dakota before then. He'd made everything easy for me, and perhaps I had unrealistic expectations of him—as well as of Mike. We had never really argued about anything before then. If anything, he likes arguing less than I do. However, living with someone is bound to bring out things you didn't anticipate.

There were a few more bumps in the road before Dakota settled down—a few more spots on the carpet, the screen door he tore in half. Carpets can be cleaned, though, and screen doors repaired. Chewed-up woodwork presents more of a challenge, and I haven't gotten around to repairing that yet—mainly, I wanted to wait and see what else fell prey to Dakota's anxiety. And to Mike's credit, he didn't press the issue.

Whatever a house may look like, a home is messy, cluttered, and lived in. Since it is likely that I will always have a dog like Dakota, no home I live in will ever be a showpiece. Mike has also grown comfortable in his new home and with all the imperfections that make it look "lived in," which are inevitable when you share your place with two dogs and three cats.

Likewise, a relationship is just as messy and cluttered as a home that's overrun with animals. My single life with Dakota was reliable, predictable. In many ways, living with Mike is anything but that. Throwing in your lot together with someone else is a leap of faith. For every tense conversation or misunderstood remark, though, there is the cup of coffee poured before you ask for it, the light left on when you come upstairs at the end of the evening, and the little dog who tries to understand what you're saying even though she's deaf and can't hear you.

Taken together, are those little reasons enough to stay? Actually, yes. In fact, what made me realize I am in this for good was mouthwash.

Mike and I get ready for bed at the same time almost every night. When I'm brushing my teeth and taking out my contact lenses, he's there at the sink doing the same. I gargle my mouthwash from a shot glass I keep on the edge of the sink. I graduated from journalism school, and journalists are known for their drinking ways; it seemed only appropriate. On the rare occasions when I'm lingering downstairs at the TV or my computer, and Mike gets upstairs before me, whenever I follow him, my shot glass is already full.

My friend Susan was right about a lot when it came to men and dogs, but not everything. There are some things for which you can't count on a dog. My choice, I realized, was not whether there was enough room in my life for both a dog and a man. My choice was whether I wanted to be patient enough and persistent enough to make both relationships work together.

The way I see it, being in a relationship is not a choice you make once and then forget, and maybe because as gay men and women who often don't have access to the traditional rituals that symbolically "seal the deal," that fluidity is much more apparent to us. It can be unnerving, but it also gives us a greater challenge to rise to our better selves. It's a choice I make every day. If I'm not choosing it every day, then I'm not really in it. And every day, I choose this house, these dogs, and this man.

· MICHAEL T. WALLERSTEIN ·

SOMETIMES YOU GET MORE

Mike Wallerstein was determined, as a thirtieth birthday present to himself, to find a dog that would embody all the characteristics of his rugged childhood Dachshund. Instead he was charmed by the runt of the litter, a piebald Dachshund with blue eyes and one white ear whom he named Bonnibelle Blue-Eyes. Mike was taken with her aloofness and independent spirit, which seemed to manifest itself in a stubborn unwillingness to learn commands and follow instructions. But there was something more, as Mike learned when a friend decided to try some experiments on her and came up with surprising results.

The problems Mike Wallerstein encountered with Bonnie are the problems at the center of a controversy in the Dachshund Club of America. One group seeks to revise the breed standard to prevent piebalds, like Bonnie, and dapples, like her sire, from competition, as a way to discourage breeding of piebalds and dapples. The concern among many breeders is that these two color patterns also carry genetic risks. Other breeders assert that responsible breeding can continue the color patterns while minimizing the risk of genetic abnormalities.

When we asked Mike to write about his relationship with Bonnie, one thing became clear: Whichever side you agree with, loving owners like Mike will not give up their dogs; they find that a dog with special needs can bring even more love into their lives.

· · · · · · · · · ·

I GREW UP with a standard red Smooth (short-haired) Dachshund named Mitzvah. She was a gift from my mother for the family in honor of my brother's thirteenth birthday. That dog became one of my best friends. She was with us from when I was six until I was twenty-one. When we put her to sleep, with the whole family there to say their goodbyes to the old girl, she was still wagging her tail. One day I knew that I'd try to get another Dachshund just like Mitzvah in the hope of recreating a little bit of that childhood bond that I'd lost, but it took me nine years to even seriously think about it. What I got was quite a bit less than what I expected, and a great deal more.

In April 2001, I got caught up in a round of corporate downsizing at my job. It had been a great job for over five years, paying for 100 percent of my M.B.A. along the way, and the new opportunity on the horizon was a silver lining. I received a good-sized severance package, so I knew that I had time to collect my thoughts. I also realized that this would be a fantastic chance to housebreak a puppy.

If only it was that simple.

I went to the local animal shelters (with my partner at the time in tow) over the course of a few weekends and came to realize that the cute little dogs, especially the Dachshund-mix pups, were usually the first ones to be adopted. We decided that we'd get a Dachshund pup from a local breeder so that I could have exactly what I wanted. After all, this was going to be my thirtieth birthday present, so we might as well do it right.

We scoured the newspaper and made a few calls to local breeders. One had mini Dachshund pups that would be weaned and ready for adoption in early July, perfect timing. She had quite a mix of colors and coats but was raving about her two piebald puppies. She said that they were rare and special. I was more interested in her red pups. If I was going to get a mini instead of a standard, it would at least need to be a shorthaired red. Already the "just like Mitzvah" plan was getting altered, but the rush of excitement was still there.

When we arrived at the breeder's house, almost two hours away in rural Illinois, she promptly led us to her available litter. I had warned my boyfriend that we needed to be careful when we picked our pup. I still had vivid memories of picking out Mitzvah from back when I was in kindergarten. My mother had a whole list of things to look for, and I would be no different.

Since I knew our pup would likely spend a lot of time alone after I found a new job, I wanted to pick one that didn't seem too needy. Imagine that: a non-needy puppy! Our goal was to pick the cutest, friendliest, most independent and confident of the litter. One thing was for sure, I did not want a piddler.

The pups were all situated under a large shade tree in the breeder's front yard, and of course they were all adorable. They were romping and playing in the grass and having a good old time in the warm spring country air. But the reds were unexpectedly blotchy instead of solid, and I didn't really like the way that they looked.

I was already beginning to regret the two-hour drive when one pup caught our attention. She was partially white, with a splash of tan on her face, in the middle of her back, and across her hindquarters and up her cute little white-tipped tail. She was like nothing I'd ever seen. We were both mesmerized.

She had one completely white ear that set off her beautiful ice-blue eyes. More importantly, she kept wandering off from the litter and exploring on her own. She didn't seem to pay any attention to the other pups unless they came over to play with her. That seemed like a very good sign based on our criteria for independence. She was plenty friendly, with her little tail wagging a mile a minute every time we approached her. That reminded me of Mitzvah more than anything.

The breeder off-handedly remarked that this unique pup carried a price premium due to her special coloring. I planned to hold onto this birthday present for a very long time, so what did I really care about a small price premium for my perfect little dog?

I later learned that this coloration was called piebald—and that the breeder was right, this pup was special. She was also the runt of the litter. Mitzvah was the runt of *her* litter. I thought, This is the pup that I have to get. We had to save the runt! Nobody ever picks the runt, but that was their loss and my gain. OK, so she peed when we greeted her, and she wasn't the right color. I was already making my mental concessions when the breeder assured us that the piddling was just a "puppy thing" as a sign of submission and that she'd grow out of it. I would just have people greet her outside on the deck or on the front porch; that would solve everything. The decision was made. None of that mattered by then anyway because I was already in love, so off we went with our prize: the funny-looking, premium-priced runt.

What should we call her? We had a bunch of cliché gay dog names, like Laverne, Shirley, or Lucy, none of which seemed to fit. She slept the whole way home, so we had two hours to come up with a moniker befitting such a little princess. Our friends Joe and Dan had a black and tan Dachshund pup named Bonnie, and I really liked that name. It seemed like a lame thing to do, but Bonnibelle Blue-Eyes is what finally stuck (Bonnie for short). How often would we run into Joe and Dan with their dog anyway?

When we got home, Bonnie received her first introduction to Boris, my twenty-pound cat. I hadn't given it any thought, but when we finally saw him side by side with Bonnie, we quickly realized that they were a matched set. He, too, was almost 100 percent white with tan points on his ears and tan stripes on his tail. I've been told that he's some rare breed of Siamese, but to me he's just the cat that I adopted from my brother.

The cat has a nervous condition that causes him to pull his hair out, which prompted his sudden departure from my brother's home at the ripe old age of two. Still, I had to marvel at the fact that I had done such a brilliant job of accessorizing my pets based on matching colors without even realizing it. Boris thought otherwise and promptly bit Bonnie on the head, barely missing her eyes. Mental note to self: Next time, read a book about bringing a new pet into the house. Who knew? Having grown up with dogs, I just assumed that Boris would take her in and show her the ropes. Instead he opted to show her his teeth.

Poor little Bonnie just looked heartbroken and ridiculous with no other dogs or pups to play with. She hunted around every corner of my home looking for her mom, her brothers, or her sisters, but then the reality of the situation set it in. She was out of her league. She was about one-tenth the size of our jealous cat and also too small to play with most of the toys we'd bought. That first night, she just moped around and looked genuinely confused. She howled all night in her crate. That broke my heart, and I worried that I'd made a mistake. Maybe we should have gotten one of her litter-mates as a playmate. All sorts of thoughts went through our minds. A howling dog will do that to a person.

Time passed and she quickly figured out that we were her new family and she grew to love everyone, even the cat. Bonnie was a one-dog comedy show. She was just as silly as could be. She always got lots of attention when we'd go for walks or to the vet because of her unusual coloring. My new buddy had arrived in grand style.

She even grew to appreciate her little crate, her safe place. She would go there when she was in trouble or if she knew she'd done something wrong. Otherwise, she would have the run of the first floor and was genuinely happy. Nighttime was a different story. Sometimes she would bark for hours, but eventually she would always fall asleep—and then we would sleep, too.

She learned how to play fetch and was a normal playful pup in every way. She was even reasonably good on a leash. The vet gave her a clean bill of health and she seemed very smart because she would use her paws to play soccer with the little mini tennis balls that we'd bought for her as toys. She was almost perfect.

However, at four months old, she still hadn't taken to her potty-training. It seemed pretty random whether she would go inside her crate, inside the house, or outside. Nothing seemed to work. My *Puppies for Dummies* book was failing me. I did everything that they said, including all of their recommended verbal commands for "getting busy" outside and lavishing her with wild praise when she would go in the right place. She mostly just seemed terrified no matter where she did her business. I wasn't too worried because I knew from experience that Dachshunds tended to be a stubborn breed.

September 2001 rolled around, and it was time for me to go back to work. Bonnie was still having accidents in her crate and around the house if we didn't let her out every hour or two. She also continued to piddle when greeting visitors. To help her make it through the day while I was at work, I enlisted the help of my friend Scott to let her out at noon.

One day he called me at work and bluntly announced, "Your dog is deaf."

When it came to her bathroom duty, she seemed to be about as bright as a fence post, but I felt the need to defend my child. I said, "No, she's not deaf, she's just stubborn, it's a Dachshund trait." He informed me that he'd been doing little experiments, like leaving the room and calling her name, or making noises while he was behind her, and she never seemed to respond. At this point, I was more than a little concerned about why one of my best friends was experimenting on my dog, but I gave him the benefit of the doubt. He further explained that something had to be wrong because she would never come back inside after being let out, even when he'd call her name repeatedly.

I didn't want it to be true, but I couldn't deny that she never seemed to hear much of anything that I said, including commands. We agreed that I would take her to the vet just to find out if anything might be wrong.

The vet's first response was that Dachshunds don't have an abnormally high incidence of deafness. He thought she was just fine. When I pushed him for a hearing test, he whistled and made a few other noises at Bonnie, one of which included snapping his fingers, after which he declared, "Yup. She's deaf."

It goes without saying that I was not impressed with his low-tech analysis. He went on to say that he couldn't be sure whether or not she was completely deaf because dogs respond to so many other things like facial expressions, vibrations, and sense of smell. He mentioned that the University of Missouri-Columbia Veterinary School could do a BAER (Brainstem Auditory Evoked Response) test to confirm her level of deafness.

Then, as an aside, he went to the back of the clinic and came back with one of his reference books on degenerative diseases. The only time that Dachshunds showed any higher-than-average frequency of deafness was through a dapple-colored sire. Bonnie's father was a dapple. My heart sank a little.

I think that I would have rather not known. She behaved quite normally and had even learned a bunch of commands, except for the difficulty in housebreaking. How could she respond to so many of my spoken commands if it was all just random? Then I remembered what the vet said about facial expressions and vibrations. I thought, Mystery solved. She always looked so confused when I would reprimand her for going to the bathroom in the house, as if she didn't even hear me coming at her. At that point, I felt pretty bad. I realized that she would never hear the sound of my voice. That's just not fair.

On my way home from the vet's office, I thought, What in the world do I need with some expensive test to tell me that my dog is deaf? I would have to take time off work, spend more money, only to find out what I already knew. It all suddenly made sense. She wasn't just stubborn—she was deaf. No amount of screaming her name out the back door would ever get her to come inside.

Then the thoughts came flooding in. She wasn't being independent when she had wandered away from her litter-mates back at the breeder's house; she couldn't even hear them! We picked her for all the wrong reasons. Here I'd gone to a breeder hoping to get a normal dog, and what I got was a sick and broken animal. I felt like I'd been given a load of damaged goods.

Of course I called the breeder right away to confront her. I told her that the vet said that Bonnie was deaf and that I wanted our money refunded in line with the health guarantee that we were given. The breeder got very defensive; she was adamant that this had never happened before. She didn't even apologize. To her, it was just business, a mistake.

Finally the breeder agreed to refund the money, but only on condition that we return Bonnie so that she could be destroyed. Suddenly all of my disappointment turned to anger. How could I let somebody hurt my deaf little baby girl? I might have been upset to learn that she was deaf, but I didn't want her to be put down.

She was so helpless, so dependent on us for everything. I had some friends who said just give her back, and others who outright forbade me from doing so. My own mother, a true dog lover, said,

"Take her back before you get attached." Too late. Sure, Bonnie was far from a normal dog, but she was worthy of my love and had already earned a place in my heart. The breeder gave me a week to make up my mind. As a concession, she countered her own offer by saying, "Bonnie will still be an otherwise healthy pet, and I guarantee that, so I will refund half of your money if you choose to keep her." Done deal, Bonnie stays.

From that point forward, I set off on a journey to learn all that I could about how to handle a deaf dog. I found an especially helpful Web site for deaf Dalmatians, which gave me the idea to teach Bonnie dog sign language. She took to it like a fish to water. She was thrilled, as was I, to finally have a way to communicate. With little effort, she learned the signs for "sit," "stay," "down," "good girl/I love you!" (her favorite), "bad girl/no" (her least favorite), "Do you want to go for a walk/outside?" "Do you want a treat/food?" (another favorite), "Do you want a drink?" and "Go to your bed/crate." Teaching her the signs was almost effortless. She'd been watching and waiting all along, and finally she could really *see* what we were saying. We eventually hung a bell by the back door so that she could ring it when she wanted to go out. It all actually worked.

She would have learned more signs, but I was exhausted and pretty much stopped there. Just knowing that she was visually oriented made life around the house so much easier. As a side effect of learning the hand signs, we could tell when she was turning her head to ignore us. It was cute to see her brain work it out. She was thinking, If I can't see their hands, they can't tell me what to do. Somewhere along the way, she even figured out the sign for "Bang! Roll over, play dead," which is by far the most adorable thing she does. By the time she was about eight months old, she was only having about one accident per week in the house.

But the quest for knowledge on Bonnie's condition didn't end there. When my mother found out about the BAER hearing test, she was convinced that it needed to be done. Even if we chose to do nothing about the lack of hearing, she wanted to know for sure. I used the cost as an excuse, but she said, "I'll help pay for it, and I'll ride down there with you." I had already earned a day of vacation after my first month of work at the new job, so I had no other excuse. I scheduled the visit to the vet school for the end of December, and Mom, Bonnie and I were on our way.

Everyone at the vet school was helpful and sympathetic. I was taught that any dog, when it isn't normally white, has a chance of being deaf in at least one ear if that ear is white. Additionally, those pretty blue eyes, when they occur in a dog that doesn't usually have them, are another genetic marker for deafness. If deafness was akin to a hand of poker, Bonnie had the makings of a royal flush. With deep regret, the vets and the techs at the school all felt like there was a very high probability that Bonnie was deaf in both ears.

However, they were still willing to do the test if I wanted to know for sure. For the test, they would use a mild sedative, attach electrodes to Bonnie's head, and then run a spectrum of sounds through both of her ears to see if there was any brainwave activity related to sound. Since we'd already made the trip, I told them to go ahead. Knowledge is power, right? It seemed pretty harmless at that point, and no harm was done.

One hour later, we were invited back into an examination room to review the results. The paperwork from the output scanner showed a flat line across all spectrums of sound: She wasn't hearing anything at any level. The undergraduate vet student holding Bonnie began to cry and kissed her gently on the head. She was still quite groggy from the anesthetic but managed to turn and lick his face.

There we were, once again feeling a sense of loss over Bonnie's deafness. We wanted so desperately to be able to "fix" her. The fact of the matter is that she was just fine with not hearing. She doesn't know a life of sound. All of that regret was going on in our heads, not hers. On the high side, they were actually impressed that a deaf Dachshund was almost completely housebroken at the age of eight months. When they framed it that way, it made me feel good, like I wasn't a total failure at raising my little dog.

Life with Bonnie has been a completely different experience from when I was a kid growing up with Mitzvah. In my eyes, Mitzvah was perfection and I loved her being so dependable. Bonnie is the epitome of imperfection, and I love her for depending on me for so much. Both dogs taught me what it means to give and receive the unconditional love of a pet. As luck would have it, they couldn't have been more different, and yet they fill up the same warm place in my heart.

In the end, I got what I wanted—and quite a bit more.

· G. RUSSELL OVERTON ·

A MOSTLY PEACEFUL EMPIRE

Any owner of multiple dogs will tell you that the

interactions among dogs are quite as complex as any

we mere humans go through with each other or

with our dogs. Dogs work out social issues such as love, anger, playfulness, and the need to establish a place in the hierarchy without any spoken language beyond barks and growls. And yet as Russ Overton demonstrates, an empire of dogs can live peacefully, even when its members vary in breed, disposition and size.

Cesar Millan, star of the National Geographic Channel's *Dog Whisperer*, believes that you must be your dog's physical and emotional leader. Often called the Dr. Phil for Dogs, he has an uncanny gift for communicating with canines. He warns that many pet owners are so eager to lavish love on their dogs that they avoid their role as leader of the pack.

Successful dog owners like Russ Overton and his partner, Bill Wisehart, recognize the need to provide leadership to their dogs along with affection, exercise, and nourishment. Their lesson to us is that multiple dogs can live together in harmony, the way Crickett, Nicky, and Carlos do, as long as their owners communicate expectations, maintain boundaries, and establish rules and routines that allow each member of the pack to know where he or she fits in.

. . . .

NICHOLAS II, JUAN Carlos I, and Crickett jointly rule the home my partner, Bill, and I have in Lansing, Michigan. It might be tempting to assume that "The Tsar of All the Russias" or "His Most Catholic Majesty" leads this triumvirate of power, but it is the untitled Crickett who reigns supreme. The irony deepens: Nicholas II, or Nicky, is a 75-pound tricolor Basset Hound, Juan Carlos I, or Carlos, is a 6-pound red-and-white Chihuahua, and Crickett is a 3-pound tricolor teacup Chihuahua. Yet with the most regal of airs Princess Crickett wields all power over both Tsar and King. This ruler of our universe proudly holds court atop a sofa cushion each day.

Nicky is the oldest. I adopted him from a breeder nearly twelve years ago when he was just six weeks old. Nicky had a severe overbite, and the breeder said that if no one adopted him, they would have to euthanize him to prevent such a defect from entering the gene pool. I appreciated the breeder's need to be responsible in protecting the breed, but with that news I could consider no other option. The breeder permitted me to adopt him on the condition I would have him neutered.

I carried him to my pickup, and we drove off together. Within seconds he began howling at the top of his lungs. I did my best to comfort him, but he wailed until the journey was done. On the way home I settled upon his name. Russian history is my academic field, so it seemed only logical to choose the name of the last reigning Russian monarch for him.

At the time I was dating a man by the name of Glenn. A year later we were virtually living together anyway and decided to end the farce of maintaining separate homes. He had adopted one of Nicky's more incorrigible subjects, a true Rasputin of dogs, a Siberian Husky named Lucy. Lucy and Nicky became good companions, and the next six years were marked with a great deal of fun and mischief.

Lucy often tempted Nicky into acts of villainy. In her constant quest for liberty, Lucy frequently found a loose board in the fence and, with Nicky in tow, enjoyed running freely through the neighborhood—sometimes at three on a crisp minus-12-degree morning. Lucy didn't care much for dog food, but she and Nicky both had a hankering for anything humans consumed. Together they hatched a scheme to pull the platters of hors d' oeuvres off the counter I had prepared for arriving guests and quickly consume the evidence before anyone could get back to the kitchen.

The dual mayhem continued until Glenn and I decided, in the year 2000, that we had other priorities in life. We had recently moved to Louisville, Kentucky, where I had no friends or social network. I found myself unattached, not happy about living in a strange place, being in my forties, and having failed at love once again.

I rejoined the dating world. I spent many Saturday evenings in smoke-filled bars, looking for Mr. Wonderful—or at least Mr. Good-Enough-for-a-Few-Hours. I dated some acquaintances from the past. I tried Internet-mating services for gay men. There I met a number of men whose physical appearance and personal character rarely matched their profile . There were times when it seemed Nicky was the only one I could trust to provide unconditional companionship.

Basset hounds are great companions. Their only challenging traits are their voracious appetites and the decibel level of their voices. Otherwise they exemplify the cliché "man's best friend." Bassets are intensely loyal and loving, and to me Nicky is the one mortal being that will always love me no matter what. To Nicky, I am the bringer of food, the one who says no a lot, who drags him into the shower, who takes him for thrilling walks where he can mark every vertical object along the way, and who knows the perfect spot on his neck to scratch.

I continued to watch the on-line postings, more for amusement than anything else. Then in early spring 2001, I noticed a profile that seemed too good to be true. His picture was handsome, and his profile said all the right things. Still, I considered the old adage "If it seems too good to be true, it probably is." After a few days the profile started gnawing at me. The words had a ring of sincerity that most on-line profiles lacked. His interests in dogs, the outdoors, and romance were not the usual cliché lines others used as a lure. I looked at the profile and the attached picture a few more times before finally deciding I had to send a response.

We decided to meet on a Saturday afternoon, April 7, 2001. Bill looked just like his on-line picture. When he saw me he smiled, and the ice around my heart melted. Within a few hours we had bonded.

Crickett was about six months old when Bill and I met. He had adopted her, also at six weeks. Her name derived from the cricket box in which Bill transported her home from the pet store.

Having overcome the initial trial of a meeting, Bill and I knew we were perfect together. We dated for a few weeks, going back and forth between our two homes. The first night at Bill's apartment Crickett selected my left shoulder as her favorite perch. At my house Nicky decided to try lap-time with Bill. Bill and I quickly fell in love with each other and with each other's dogs.

Our biggest concern was how a fat Basset Hound and a tiny Chihuahua would get along. Theoretically Nicky could sit on Crickett and crush her to death or mistakenly think she was a small rodent and chase her as prey. With great hesitation and knowing full well that the outcome of the meeting could determine the course of the relationship, Bill and I decided it was time to introduce Crickett and Nicky.

It worked. Nicky was happy to meet a companion who was much lower maintenance than Lucy had been. Crickett was happy to meet a companion whose fat belly could keep her warm. Their first meeting was not unlike that of their daddies. They sniffed each other's butts, licked each other all over, and snuggled up together. They became instant companions.

It was spring and perfect weather for a love affair to blossom. Among our many outdoor activities, we frequently took Crickett and Nicky for walks in the park. Passersby sometimes commented, "What an odd pair!" We were never sure whether the remark was targeted at us or the dogs. Odd couples or not, the four of us had forged a family unit by the end of summer.

We moved several times together over the next few years, including back to Lansing at the request of my former employer there. Bill was able to obtain a transfer with his company. We finally settled into a 1950s split-level house in a Lansing neighborhood that gay and lesbian couples have been restoring for nearly twenty years. We have made our own contribution to the effort.

Crickett established her status as household alpha, and she secured genuine imperial status through the bequest of a priceless collar of jewels. One Halloween a human friend of most royal rank for the evening removed his bracelet and performed the coronation by fastening it around Crickett's neck. Like Cinderella's slipper, it was a perfect fit.

Though Nicky was much older and much larger, he deferred to Crickett's authority. It is possible that Bill and I unwittingly encouraged her status. Nicky enjoys lap-time and seizes the opportunity whenever he can, but Crickett always has priority. From her perch on my left shoulder she can survey her realm from on-high. Nicky could never do that. Besides, his realm is really outdoors. There he can always find the scent of a "kitty-cat," buried treasure, or, his favorite, pond water. Crickett only enjoys the outdoors if it is hot, dry, sunny, and humans are present. The idea of getting her feet wet in a puddle or tripping through moist grass is anathema to her—ever the princess.

Bill, Crickett, Nicky, and I lived as a happy family unit for a few years. Then, like an unexpected pregnancy, Juan Carlos arrived. One snowy March Sunday two lesbian friends called from two blocks away saying they had a surprise. In their hands was a four-week-old Chihuahua puppy. His eyes were barely open, and he wasn't ready for solid food. In the course of three days he had been passed to three homes, all rejecting this helpless yet loveable critter.

I was not thrilled about the idea of another animal responsibility, but I recognized the crisis. He needed a loving family. Bill never felt hesitation in the matter. I knew we were keeping the puppy, but I made it conditional upon me having the honor of giving him a name. That he would be regal was a given, but it would have made no sense to have two tsars in the house. Using the best logic I could muster, I theorized that because he was a Chihuahua and the province by that name was formerly a part of the Spanish Empire, he should carry the name of a Spanish monarch. My next dilemma was whether the name should be historic or contemporary. Franco (who was merely a dictator) was never under consideration. Of Spanish rulers in the past 500 years, the current ruler seems to me to be the best example of what a monarch should be. Therefore, I settled on Juan Carlos I as an appropriate name for our new puppy.

The ensuing years were a challenge in our family. Nicky and Crickett were downright hostile to the introduction of another monarch into their presence. No motherly instincts stirred Crickett, and when Carlos thought Nicky's long, floppy ears were a chew-toy, Nicky let out a rare growl of warning. Carlos made matters worse by chewing holes in socks, underwear, sheets, hats, leather coats, and anything else left on the floor or a chair for more than ten minutes.

But his green eyes, constantly licking tongue, endless curiosity, and loving demeanor ultimately won all hearts in the house. Crickett found a playmate closer to her size. When Carlos crawled upon Nicky's back, it was like a Japanese geisha's back rub, but with claws that scratched nicely.

Carlos is now two years old. With Nicky at twelve and Crickett at six, Carlos is the most energetic and playful being in the house. Sometimes he and Nicky play tug-of-war, which always ends in a Russian victory over the Spanish crown. Sometimes they chase each other around the house, Carlos making about twelve passes for every one of Nicky's. And sometimes, Crickett and Carlos end up in a wrestling match; Carlos usually loses there too, but it appears to be out of deference to Crickett's status as the alpha.

Carlos also goads Bill and me into playing with him. We toss Carlos's stuffed animal for him to chase. He runs after the toy at top speed, skidding to a stop on the terrazzo floor, often bumping into a wall, only to repeat the process a few dozen times before Bill or I grow weary of the game. Carlos never tires of it.

On any given Saturday evening, Bill is ready for bed long before I am. He asks, "Who wants to go to bed?"—the all-important question Crickett has been waiting hours to hear—and she jumps up and runs upstairs. Bill places her on the bed, she twirls around five times, then darts under the covers, not to be seen again until daylight.

After Bill and Crickett snuggle into bed, I warm up the sound system, and Ella Fitzgerald belts a flawless tune from a vintage LP. While I sip a snifter of Scotch, Carlos wraps himself around my neck until it is time to turn the record. Nicky sits at my side with the only free hand stroking his head. Eventually Ella's concert is over. The lights go out, and Nicky and I walk up the stairs, me carrying Carlos because he is too sleepy to make it on his own. A goodnight kiss, a snuggle with Bill, and I drift off to sleep, knowing that all is well in the realm where Tsar, King, and Princess can sleep in peace.

WHAT WE LEARN FROM OUR DOGS

· VICTOR J. BANIS ·

THE GIRLS

Victor Banis experienced a special kind of communication with his dogs, particularly with Jenny, his first. You don't have to be a psychic to know what your dog is feeling or to communicate your own emotions and expectations. But you do have to learn to listen to your dog—which means being sensitive, using your intuition, and allowing yourself to really feel what your dog feels.

People often establish this connection with other people: couples who finish each other's sentences, mothers who know, with no spoken communication, what their babies need or want. But the same kind of connection is possible with our dogs. And what we communicate to them, they, in turn, are able to communicate to each other, just as Jenny taught Prima to be housebroken and to walk off the leash.

One of the pioneers of gay literature, Banis was persecuted in the 1960s by the U.S. government on federal charges of conspiracy to distribute obscene material simply because his first novel, *The Affairs of Gloria*, dared to depict lesbian life. When we asked him to write about the dogs in his life, he gave us this essay about the two dogs he and his friends called "the girls." Prima and Jenny had a relationship as close as any human couple's, sharing an admirably deep love. His keen novelist's eye captures every nuance of that relationship, from its beginning to its end.

· · · · · · · · · ·

THEIR NAMES WERE Jenny and Prima, but everyone called them "the girls." They were lovers, of a sort; lesbians perhaps, though I can't really say if their affectionate cuddling, nestling, licking, and mounting ever produced any kind of orgasm. I can't even say if it was sexual in nature. I do know that Prima would lie for hours in rapture, eyes closed, a dreamy smile on her face, while Jenny patiently cleaned her ears; and sometimes at night I would hear noises—long, languorous sighs, or a happy panting that sounded suspiciously like girlish laughter—from the floor beside my bed, but I never peeked. Everyone is entitled to a little privacy.

Prima, painfully shy, was clearly the femme, a pretty, mostly Shepherd mix with no pedigree but gracious manners. Jenny, a registered Springer who seemed aware of her superiority to the unregistered rest of us, was the aggressive member of our ménage, an in-your-face sort, although she could be sweet and even demure when she chose.

They were both bright and clever. They did none of the usual doggish tricks, however. I am always astonished to see dogs roll over on command, or beg, or walk on their hind legs—all of which would have been too showoffy for Prima, and which Jenny would have disdained as beneath her dignity. In any case, I could never have managed to teach the girls such tricks. Truth to tell, I never managed to teach them much of anything. Jenny was self-taught in all matters concerning deportment, and Prima was Jenny-taught, by a system the secret of which entirely eluded me.

Jenny was with me first. When I went to the breeder's home to pick a puppy from the litter, her brothers and sisters were busy across the pen, but Jenny dashed over to greet me and to announce that I had been chosen for her future partner. I took her home that evening, and by the next morning she had housebroken herself.

I did try to teach her about leashes, but she was not fond of being paraded around on a chain like the inferior partner in some bondage relationship. She made it clear on our first day at it that she could walk perfectly well beside me on her own, and if I wanted her to heel, I had only to snap my fingers and she would do so as well as any dog in a show ring, thank you very much. So we gave up leashes, except in those places where they were required by ordinance. She seemed to understand the difference, and would behave perfectly well while on one, but with a certain long-suffering attitude and the occasional huff of impatience.

I came to believe that she was able to divine, by some super sense, what it was that I wanted, and so could do it without actual training. Certainly I never met anyone, dog or human, with whom I shared such an uncanny rapport. There was the time, for instance, during her puppyhood, when she developed a penchant for eating things. She never quite got over that, and throughout most of her life regarded anything that didn't bark back at her or run faster than she could as fair game for a snack.

On this occasion, she ate a palm tree. It was only a small one, admittedly, in a little pot on the floor by the window, where I thought it would be encouraged to grow into something large and lush and add a certain opulence to my not-very-elegant decor.

I don't mean that she ate a leaf or two. I mean, she ate it: leaves, trunk, roots, everything but the pot and the soil. It seemed to do her no lasting damage, but you have never known dog gas until yours has devoured a palm tree.

I discussed this chewing issue with her breeder, afraid of what might succumb next to her peculiar appetite, and the breeder said, "You must surprise her at it, and scold her while she is in the act."

That sounded reasonable enough. I left her home alone the next afternoon, got in the car, slamming the door loudly for her benefit, drove several blocks away, and parked. Then I stole back to the house, crawled around the corner (literally on hands and knees), and lifted my head to look in through the den window—and found Jenny staring directly at me with an amused expression. All in all, I thought it wiser just to buy no more palm trees.

There were demonstrations aplenty, however, of her eerie gift of knowing where I was and what I was doing. In those days I often visited a publisher far out in the San Fernando Valley, and I would usually stop for lunch at a coffee shop on the way, leaving Jenny in the car, and taking a window table so I could keep an eye on her. With her head out the window of the car, she would turn left, turn right, left again and right again, using some sort of radar to slowly zero in on my location. The coffee shop windows were darkly tinted; it was impossible to see in from outside. Yet within a few minutes she would be staring directly at me with a look of extreme annoyance, and her gaze would not waver until lunch was finished and I returned to the car with abject apologies and, needless to say, some sort of payoff for neglecting her.

She was a year old when a boyfriend—mine, not hers—arrived one day carrying in his arms a peculiar-looking little animal that purported to be a German Shepherd with the ears of a jackrabbit.

Her name, he informed me, was Prima, and she had been terribly abused in her previous home. I pointed out that I had neither the desire nor the room for a second pet, and reminded him that my landlord had not been happy about the first one, but he asked plaintively if I would just keep her for a day or so while he found a home for her. I made the mistake of saying yes.

In all fairness, he did warn me that she was not yet housebroken. By the next morning, however, Jennie had seen to that, and they were going outside together. That struck me as even more mysterious, since it was not the sort of oddity you would expect to have happen twice. Still, I had no reason to complain.

Since we lived in the city, I tried training the newcomer to a leash, thinking that Jennie's instant understanding of that necessity was certainly not likely to repeat itself, as the toilet training had. But Prima was such a frightened little thing that, no sooner had you put any kind of collar around her neck than she fell to the floor in a quivering, peeing mass and could not be induced to regain her feet until the collar was removed and she had been reassured that no physical violence was intended.

It was Jenny once again who took charge. To my astonishment, by the next day she had taught Prima to heel at the snap of my fingers, and from then on I could walk down a busy sidewalk in, say, West Hollywood, with both girls safely and politely at perfect heel.

How had Jenny done that? What secret language had passed between them? I only knew that whatever I wanted her to do Jenny divined, and whatever Jenny did Prima did as well. So I could come out of the kitchen into the den, where the rug had just been shampooed, and walk around the bare-floor perimeter to cross the room, and Jenny would follow after me, and Prima after her, and not a paw upon the damp rug. I could entertain less–dog enthusiastic guests in the living room and, though the girls had the run of the house, they would sit politely in the doorway while I sipped cocktails with the guests. I have had two-legged friends whose manners weren't so good.

They could be parted from me only by trickery. If, of necessity, I left them home without me, they would sit at the upstairs window and cry in great mournful howls until I returned, to be greeted with wagging tails and scathing looks.

The girls shared my life for fifteen happy and loving years. About halfway through that span, we moved to a cabin in the mountains. They loved it: the great outdoors, exploring together, creeks to splash in, all sorts of scents to investigate. In the summer we took long treks in the woods; in the winter, they liked me to throw snowballs for them to catch. They got friendly with the squirrels, who lost their fear of the girls and would leap over Prima when she slept in the doorway to come inside and beg for a snack. Jenny was a jumper, and would dash over the most astonishing obstacles while I gaped open-mouthed. Prima liked to run because it was something at which she could beat both of us, since I was slow and Jenny, incurably curious, was forever distracted. Prima was not much of a swimmer, but Jenny the spaniel would plunge with delight into any stream, pond, or pool, although a single raindrop on her nose was enough to cut short a walk beyond the bare necessity of business.

Prima discovered that the field mice were afraid of her, and it bolstered her self-esteem that someone thought her ferocious. Not so very ferocious, however. She came home one day with what appeared to be an odd case of the mumps, her cheeks swollen grotesquely. She came directly to me and began to disgorge from her mouth one, two, three, six in all, baby bunnies, obviously newborn, quite unharmed. She had brought them home for me to raise, apparently—no doubt having innocently terrified their desolate mother into abandoning them. Jennie regarded these blind, helpless intruders with scorn, but Prima stayed close and watched with hopeful eye as I did my best to save her orphans. It was to no avail, however. She seemed to grieve when I buried them in a box in the backyard, and Jenny sat dutifully, if unmoved.

Jenny still ate shamelessly, preferably people food: the stem ends of tomatoes, pieces of carrots or celery, pie or cake—if it was on my plate or in my hand, it was surely meant for her as well, as she saw it. If a visitor left a strawberry daiquiri sitting on the floor by her chair, she would shortly find her glass mysteriously empty, and Jenny would sport a pink moustache. Prima, on the other hand, would eat and drink only proper dog things. If I attempted to test her by hiding a couple of green peas in her kibble, the bowl would be licked clean, the peas untouched in its bottom.

The years passed, and we all got older. Jenny went mostly blind, and did not hear well, and had a bad back from all that youthful jumping. She liked to doze on the deck in the afternoon sun, and Prima and I would sit guard to watch for any hungry coyotes, who tended to look at Jenny as something desirous to be taken home for dinner and would sometimes steal close to extend the invitation.

Prima got a little gray around the snout, and her hip bothered her when the weather got cold, but otherwise she remained frisky and looked quite young for her years. She had finally grown into those jackrabbit ears and was quite a handsome little devil.

They would not sleep in my bed, even when invited in the dead of winter, but they must be right next to it on the floor—together, of course. When Jenny stumbled one night and fell down the stairs from the loft bedroom, I made my bed on the living room floor in front of the fireplace, and that was where the three of us slept afterward. Jenny sometimes snored. Prima liked to have me warm my feet on her back.

As a result, no doubt, of her reckless eating, Jenny developed a stomach tumor, which had to be removed—with much trepidation on my part because the doctor warned that surgery was iffy at her age. She survived, but I began to worry about her mortality. She was fifteen now, Prima fourteen. That was old for dogs of their size.

Astonishingly, it was Prima, who had always seemed the

picture of health, whom I lost first. She got a fever, sudden and severe. I rushed her to the hospital, and the doctor put her on an intravenous solution to combat the dehydration, and I left her with him. He called me the next morning to say we had lost her.

Her death was painful to me, but watching Jenny over the next few weeks was nearly unbearable. Carson McCullers says that there is a lover and a beloved, and that they come from different countries. No one outside of any relationship can ever know its intricacies, and certainly theirs was beyond my ken, but I had always had the impression that in this pairing Jenny was the beloved and Prima the lover.

I said before that their relationship was lesbian in nature, but I have no doubt some would argue that it was really more a matter of "sisters." That may well be, but of one thing there can be no argument: it was love, as profound as any celebrated by bard or songsmith.

Jenny spent her first day alone searching the house for her beloved friend; concluding finally that Prima was truly gone, she stopped eating. Jenny, who had sometimes seemed to live to eat, never ate again.

At the doctor's advice, I tried to force-feed her. As soon as my hand was gone, back up came everything that I had managed to get down. Nothing, none of her favorite foods, would tempt her. She went outside for business, but she had no interest any longer in our walks in the woods. She would rest on my lap and welcome my petting, but of gladness she showed not a trace. Her once-happy tail was still.

With each day, she got thinner and weaker, while my heart broke for her. And finally, all too soon, the morning came when she could no longer stand, her emaciated legs too weak to support her. I held her and stroked her head, and whispered things to her that many would no doubt think foolish. I could only hope that, as so often in the past, she understood what was on my mind and in my heart.

Without the girls, I no longer cared for the cabin in the woods. I moved back to the city. Some weeks later I ran into an old friend, who asked after the girls.

"They're gone," I told him, "Prima died of a sudden fever. And Jenny died of a broken heart."

That was years ago, but I still wake sometimes in the night, and think I hear a happy panting on the floor by my bed, and I will reach to pet them, and find no one there.

Then I lie in the darkness, remembering; after a time, I dry my eyes, and go back to sleep, and dream of the girls.

· JACK MORTON ·

PERFECT COMPATIBILITY

When Jack Morton decided to share his comfortable Georgia home with a puppy, it was the first step on a lifelong discovery of how rich interspecies friendship can be. He retraced for me the path from the initial joy of naming his new friend, to the shared comfort of middle age with his current dogs.

Jack juggles the demands of an increasingly successful hair-styling career with the need to love, cherish, and make a home for his partner and the other couple in their household, two elegant and exuberant Shih Tzus. When the men made a decision to expand their business interests to run a high-end gift store near their second home in the Blue Ridge Mountains, a question arose. How could they run separate businesses in separate cities and still share the company of dogs who both feel are necessary to their existence? The answer is a dilemma with which they still struggle.

Jack spoke with me in interviews from his Atlanta home and from his luxurious salon about both the practical and the inexplicable benefits of including dogs in the family.

· · · · · · · · · ·

MY FIRST DOG was a tiny Shih Tzu puppy, and the name on his papers read, "Baron Security." When I first brought him home, I took him outside, and said, "Come on, little one, let's go."

"Little One" fit him so well, the name stuck. I spelled it "Liddlewun."

When Liddlewun was about three, I got a second Shih Tzu named Blake. Those two dogs were devoted to each other and spent every minute together.

I had always had dogs as a kid, but I don't think I appreciated them as much as I do as an adult. I think it has to do with the fact that I don't have children. My dogs are my children. They are such a part of my life, and I'm devoted to them. The vet tells me, "Your dogs live on love."

I have a wonderful salon in Atlanta called Indulgence, and I get called a lot to work on press junkets when people are coming through town: Jane Fonda, Barbara Walters, Peter Jennings, Laura Linney, Alfre Woodard. I'm even on television myself; I do a makeover segment on the local NBC affiliate. Viewers send in letters telling why they need a makeover, and I transform them. I've been doing it for about twenty years.

One day I was working at my salon, and I got a hysterical phone call from my housekeeper. I had a fenced-in area at the back of my house, but for some reason the gate was open and she didn't know it.

She said, "I can't find Blake!"

I immediately left the salon, drove home, and started looking everywhere for him. I was terrified that he would go into the street and be run over. When they're used to being with you all the time, they don't know anything about traffic.

He wasn't in the street, so I thought that somebody must have picked him up. I had flyers printed up, and I put them everywhere. For twenty-four hours I was a disaster. I didn't go to work the next day. My appointments are booked a year ahead, so it's big trouble if I don't go in.

Two days went by, and I was just frantic. I was everywhere, asking every business owner, going door to door in the neighborhood.

Finally I got a phone call from my vet. He said, "Jack, did you lose Blake?"

I said, "Oh, my god, do you have him? Is he OK? Was he injured?"

He said, "I have a lady here who brought him in, and she says he's her dog. She wants me to give him all his shots. But I know it's Blake. I need you to come here."

The assistant told the woman something like "We're doing some tests, and you have to wait for the results."

I drove there like a madman. I walked in, and the moment Blake saw me, he went crazy. I told the woman, who was very well-dressed and in her forties, "This is my dog."

She said that didn't prove anything, they all look alike, and he's a friendly dog.

I said, "OK, but he has a growth behind his ear that we've been watching. The doctor is going to do surgery and take it off."

They looked, and of course it was there.

She was so angry. She said, "This is my dog. I brought him in for his shots."

I said, "You found that dog."

Finally she admitted that she had found him. But she said, "He was abandoned!"

That made me furious. I said, "Ma'am, look at him. He is a healthy, well-cared-for animal. He was not living out on the street like a homeless person. He is certainly not abandoned. There are signs up all over this area."

If it had been any other vet besides my vet, I would have never seen Blake again. He would have been gone.

As she was leaving, she commented to me that she had also found her last dog running loose. This is a woman who lived in my neighborhood and drove a Mercedes. I thought to myself, *Was it a purebred that you picked up somewhere when someone turned their back?* It infuriated me. I thought, How dare you?

When Liddlewun was diagnosed with cancer, I told my partner, Michael, that I wanted a third dog. He said, "Absolutely not. We do not need another dog."

I said, "I can't imagine having just one dog." I couldn't imagine one of them being alone.

On my birthday, March 11, I was walking through the mall, and in the pet store window was a little black and white Shih Tzu. I'd always gotten my Shih Tzus from a breeder. I know you're not supposed to get dogs from pet stores. But I went in and asked if I could see the dog. The assistant put me in a private room, where you're supposed to play with the dog for a few minutes to see if you want to buy it.

I stayed for two hours.

Michael worked at a Lexus dealership. While I was playing with the dog, Michael's boss and his wife came into the store. I said, "What are you doing here?"

They said, "We're buying some toys for our dogs. What are you doing here?"

I said, "Well, I'm just looking at this little dog."

Michael's boss said, "You've got to have that dog. That is a beautiful dog."

He bought a stuffed, squeaky octopus, handed it to me, and said, "Here's his first toy."

I went ahead and bought him, even though it was against Michael's wishes. The only way I could think to break the news to Michael was to name him Lexus.

I went to the dealership, and I had Lexus in my inside coat pocket. Michael came out and said, "What are you doing here?"

I said, "Oh, I just came to visit."

His boss said, "He bought a Lexus."

Michael said, "What?"

I said, "I did. I bought a Lexus."

He said, "If you bought a Lexus from any other dealership except this one, we need to talk."

I said, "I did buy a Lexus." And I opened my coat.

Michael looked at me and said, "You did not buy that animal."

"I did."

Michael was so upset that he would not speak to me. When he came home, he would not have anything to do with Lexus. But he was such a little puppy, and so playful, that he just stole Michael's heart. Liddlewun and Blake were eighteen and fifteen, respectively. They were definitely part of the family, but they weren't into hiding under the couch and running around the house the way Lexus did. Lexus is such a sweet dog who could win anyone over.

In twenty-four hours Lexus was Michael's dog. Michael said, "OK, OK, I was wrong. He's beautiful and I love him."

Lexus's next challenge was to win over the two older dogs. Liddlewun and Blake were so established in their routines that he had to make his way very carefully. He would run at them and try to play with them. But they had no interest. They looked at him like, "Who are you? You're so little. You don't even look like us. We don't know why you're here."

But after a while they started to say, "OK, you want to play?" Lexus put so much life back into the other dogs.

And it was a good thing, because Liddlewun passed, and Blake and Lexus became best friends. In the beginning, when Liddlewun had just died, Blake really needed Lexus. And Lexus understood it. As much as he wanted to be crazy and run around, he would comfort Blake and let Blake rest his head on his shoulders. For a few minutes. Then he made Blake get up and play with him.

Two years later, Blake was diagnosed with cancer. We would all miss him so much, but Michael and I had each other. When Blake died, Lexus would be alone. He would lose his best buddy, and I didn't want that.

I think it's important that if you are going to take on the responsibility of an animal, you give him the best care possible, just as you would a child. So I knew I had to get Lexus a friend. I decided to go to the supposed number-one breeder in the state. I called and asked if she had any males for sale.

She said, "Yes, I have two left in the litter, and they will be available in one more week."

I drove and drove and drove; it was a couple of hours away. There were two absolutely beautiful dogs—very, very small. The female had already been promised, but the male was available.

The husband jokingly told me that the male was a spider monkey. He's a brindle color, and he has the most beautiful face, almost like a little monkey.

I took him home. He was so tiny that he fit in the palm of my hand. He weighed less than one pound. I called him Trés Bien, French for "very good," or Trey for short. I took him to the vet, and she was crazy about him. She said, "I've got to have one of these dogs. I want to buy one for my parents. It's the most beautiful little dog I've ever seen in my life."

He was in perfect health. About a month later, I took him in for his checkup and shots. I said to the vet, "You know, he seems different from any Shih Tzu I've ever had. His hair hasn't started growing up between his eyes." That's the long hair that you can pull up into a ponytail.

She said, "Well, he's the runt of the litter, he's very small, and I think it's going to take him a while before he starts to grow."

I waited, and about a month later I took him back. By then I was worried. I told her, "Maybe something's wrong with him. His hair still hasn't started growing."

She said, "There's nothing wrong with him. Except that he's not a Shih Tzu."

"What!"

"He is definitely not a Shih Tzu. I think he's a Tibetan Spaniel."

"Wait a minute. I just received his papers in the mail. He is a 100 percent registered AKC Shih Tzu. There were his parents names and numbers and all the registration information!"

She said, "I'm telling you he's a Tibetan Spaniel."

I went home and looked up the breed on the internet. She was right; my dog looked exactly like a Tibetan Spaniel.

What should I do? I had wanted a Shih Tzu, but I was so in love with this little dog! Besides, he had taken full command of the household.

I tried to reach the breeder, but she never returned my calls. . .

There was never any thought of returning him because he is the most adorable animal. He and Lexus are so close; they sleep nose to nose in the same bed. They play and roll around on the floor. They are so compatible.

When I introduced Trey into the pack, he brought life back to Blake and Lexus. There was this young puppy, so full of energy, and the other dogs seemed to think, OK, we'll go along with this until he leaves.

But of course he never left.

Trey is now two and a half years old. What blew my mind was that he is so agile. He can jump from the floor to the back of the sofa exactly like a cat.

This dog has so many toys. But he is organized; he has a system. When he gets up in the morning, he takes every toy out from the bedroom to the living room. They stay there all day long, and he takes turns, playing with each toy. At night, about nine-fifteen, he starts collecting and transporting them to the bedroom. It's almost like he knows when it's time to put his toys away.

If Trey's toy rolls underneath the sofa or a chair where he can't get it, he will sit and look at you and talk and talk and talk. He'll go to the sofa, look underneath, and look up at you. He'll do this again and again until he gives you this frustrated look that says, "Why don't you get it?"

He's not barking. He's trying to speak.

He looks like a raccoon. His fur is a dark golden with a lot of black, and a red tone under his eyes and his face, like a mask. And on his legs and tail, he has almost like feathers. If you look at him walking from behind, he looks like he has on a pair of chaps.

The dogs have grown up with our handful of friends as their family. When any friend comes to the door, they get so excited. Trey will run and get a toy and bring it out, like he's saying, "Here's a present!" He gives each guest one of his toys.

He's so curious that he would follow anyone. I put a special set of tags on him that I had custom-made. It says, "My name is Trés Bien. If I have left home, it was not because I wanted to. I need to get back. There will be a huge reward." And I put all of my phone numbers.

When they sleep, they sleep on their backs. And they snore! They sleep in the bed with me. I would never think of telling them that they have to sleep on the floor. They know the routine.

Michael and I had our home in Atlanta for fifteen years. Some very dear friends of ours wanted to buy a cabin, and they found this town in north Georgia called Blue Ridge. It's so quaint, almost like Mayberry. It has a train depot, bike races, fishing competitions, concerts in the park, antique shops, log cabins and trail riding. They celebrate Smokey the Bear's birthday like it's a national holiday.

We just fell in love with it and bought our home there. About a year ago I said to Mike, "We need to open a business in this town." It was getting ready to explode. We bought a business in downtown Blue Ridge called Wrapsody in Blue. It's a gift store with very high-end furniture and gifts. It's been such a huge success that Michael moved there full time. It's only about an hour and fifteen minutes from Atlanta.

The dogs stay in the mountains with Michael. I'd love to move there full time, but to walk away from Indulgence would be kind of foolish at fifty years old. In Blue Ridge, Lexus and Trey have four acres where they can run. Mike can take them with him to the store with him, which is the perfect environment for them. They love the people coming in. They can walk around the store or just lay down and chill out.

But I miss them horribly. I call them every night. Mike puts me on the speaker phone and I ask them how their day went. They actually respond. Mike said they always start looking at the door, as if saying, "Where is he? We don't see him."

Dogs have a such a good sense of time. When I was up in Blue Ridge, I realized that at about six o'clock Trey would go to the front door and sit. And he would not move until Mike pulled up. He knew it was time for him to come home.

I think it's a sense that we as human beings aren't aware of. It's an internal, mysterious skill, like the way they know a storm is coming. Lexus is terrified of thunder. He'll come and jump in my lap, looking at me like, "Something is going to happen." And, sure enough, within about thirty minutes we'll have a thunderstorm.

The dogs have taught me about togetherness, about what it's like being part of a couple. When you find your friend, you know it. We're a family, but inside of the family, they're a couple. They are uniquely attuned to one another's needs. It's a goal, to be that attuned. Like knowing when someone's coming home, and when the sky is about to break apart with thunder. They have that perfect compatibility. Maybe it's another thing we humans can't know.

· HAL CAMPBELL ·

BABE, MY THREE-LEGGED HERO

Many dog lovers believe that dogs were placed on

earth to teach us lessons—lessons about love, loyalty,

and loss. Hal Campbell's Beagle, Babe, had lessons to

teach in abundance. Suffering from the complications of
AIDS and the side effects of the drugs, Hal thought that he
had the market locked on suffering—until he found a lump
behind Babe's head. The way she jumped at every chance to
enjoy life—even after she lost a leg—inspired Hal to apply
that same gusto to his own life, and to dedicate himself to
loving more Beagles after Babe, even though he knows these
dogs may outlive him.

Dog ownership can provide many health benefits, from lower blood pressure to higher levels of serotonin. Studies have also shown that dogs can reduce stress levels in doctors' and dentists' offices. Pet-therapy programs exist at many hospitals around the country, helping patients recover more quickly and in better spirits.

In San Francisco, people whose doctors believe a pet can improve the quality of their lives can officially register their dogs with the Animal Care and Control Agency as "assistance dogs." Just like the canine companion of someone visually impaired, an assistance dog has the legal right to ride on the bus or in a taxi and to go into shops, restaurants and public buildings. The dog must be trained in some way that helps the patient—and that training can be as simple as licking the face of someone who's depressed. Since beginning this registry in 1998, the City by the Bay has seen a big jump in the number of those who recognize how a dog can help those suffering from any impairment to their health--even something as invisible as high blood pressure or HIV infection.

. . . .

BABE STARED OUT the patio window and watched the rain splatter against the glass. Her posture was as perfect as it could be—considering that she only had three legs. What was she thinking? Were her thoughts focused on those years when she was young, healthy, and filled with boundless energy, eager to chase a ball or play tug-of-war over the bedraggled little stuffed bear that she protected so fiercely when she wasn't chewing on it? Or did she wonder why all that pain was coursing through her body?

Whatever her thoughts, when she turned away from the window after her long vigil, she focused her full attention on me. She sat a few feet from my recliner and tilted her head slightly. It was as if she was saying, "I know you hurt, too. I'm so sorry we can't wrestle on the floor or go for walks like the old days. But we still have each other, and that's all that really counts."

Of course, I knew that a certain amount of her attention toward me was motivated by her insatiable appetite. So with great effort I pushed the foot-rest-release pedal on the side of the recliner, grabbed my cane, and then forced myself upright. As I shuffled toward the kitchen, Babe followed, hopping on her remaining three legs like an excited rabbit.

She never let me go into the kitchen alone, since she knew she had a fifty-fifty chance of getting a treat. I lifted the ceramic lid off the treat jar and retrieved a "gourmet" biscuit shaped like a fire hydrant. (The biscuits were truly labors of love baked by a friend whose landlord didn't allow pets.) I used to make her sit before I gave her a treat. But it became hard for her to maintain her balance due to the missing leg. She was no longer my personal circus performer. She got the treat for just simply being. Why make the surviving of daily life any harder than it needs to be?

Surviving is something with which I am on intimate terms. In 1995, after enduring a long period of fatigue and weight loss, I got a complete physical examination. When all the blood-test results came back, the diagnosis was conclusive: AIDS. The survival prognosis for most AIDS patients then was only eighteen months after beginning treatment. At that time I had two Beagles, and after I came out of my shell-shocked state, I thought about what would become of them after I was gone. But my fears about their future were soon put to rest when my two dearest friends— the "parents" of a Beagle acquired after they saw the pleasure I got from mine—assured me that they would gladly become a three-Beagle family.

Two months later, the first of the protease inhibitors came out and I was one of the first patients to begin treatment with it. The long-term effects of the drugs were not known, but at that time the greatest focus was on extending a patient's lifespan. A decade has now passed and I am still here. However, some of those early drugs did terrible damage to my liver. Now I need a new one, but because of my overall poor health, I can't get approval for placement on a transplant waiting list. (You can be sick; you just can't be too sick!) So now I'm biding my time until the end comes. But I have had a wonderful life, and the Beagles who have passed through it have been a major source of all the joy I have known.

Maude, my first Beagle (named after a great-grandmother) arrived in 1969—a gift from a coworker whose Beagle couple had produced an unplanned litter. She brightened my life for nearly eighteen years, and when she died in 1987, I understood what people meant when they said they had lost their best friend. But by then I had learned of an organization that matched unwanted Beagles with people like me. I went to a dog show at the San Francisco Cow Palace and registered at a booth sponsored by the Beagle Rescue Society. Soon I got a call about a Beagle at the Alameda shelter. She had been found with no ID and was available for adoption. That was Cassie, followed by Claire, and then Chloe.

It was Chloe I mourned for prior to Babe's entrance into my life. By the time I was ready to open my heart to a new Beagle, the world had moved into the age of the personal computer. So instead of scanning newspaper ads or trekking from shelter to shelter, I merely had to log on to the Internet to check out the current residents being cared for by various animal shelters and rescue organizations. I found the site for the Sacramento SPCA and came upon Babe's picture. I called and learned she was still homeless.

Soon I was driving two hours to meet the Beagle whom I hoped would share my bed just like all those others before her. A volunteer brought her out to the waiting room. I wish that I could say that she leaped into my lap, but she couldn't have been less impressed with me. She was far more interested in sniffing the rear ends of the other dogs in the room. But finally the novelty of that task wore off, and she began to acknowledge my presence. Although her aloof attitude irked me, at the same time I found it fascinating. This was going to be a unique relationship.

Nearly a year passed with the two of us maintaining our "landlord/tenant" relationship. Then one night while I was reading in bed, I had the sensation of being watched. I lowered my book and saw Babe staring at me. She was sitting up between my legs about three feet away. She cocked her head in each direction, and then, after another moment of intense staring, she leaped up and licked me—once. It was as if a light bulb had gone on in her head: "Oh, I get it. I'm here to stay. You're not going to get rid of me like the people before you did." And from that moment on, Babe was a different dog. We had finally bonded. We were best buds.

But every relationship endures some bad times. I thought my health issues would be the stumbling block in Babe's and my lives. One day, however, while stroking Babe's fur I felt a lump on her back just behind her head. This motivated me to intently examine the rest of her body and I found another lump—smaller than the first—right near the joint where her front left leg connected to her torso. The next day I took her to my vet who X-rayed her. The films revealed that the tumors were malignant.

Thus began the battle that was to last for nearly a year. Tumors popped out on Babe's body like toadstools on a tree stump. At first some were excised, but when the wounds didn't heal and her hair grew back at a rate so slow that it was hardly visible, injections of toxins to kill the malignant cells became the procedure of choice.

Then came the day when the dreaded word "amputation" was used in conversation for the first time. Following its initial excision, the tumor on the joint on her front leg had grown back. Since the tumor was now the size of a plum, it was decided that a repeat surgery would be a futile gesture. "The leg should go," the vet said quietly and emphatically. I thought of all the dogs and cats I had seen getting around just fine with only three legs. I was sure Babe would overcome such a limitation, but when I saw the bandaged bloody stump after the surgery, I confess I questioned my agreement to the surgery. However, within a couple of days Babe was hopping around the house, just as curious as ever about what was going on in her little world. As for her appetite, her motto was still, "Eat first and ask questions later."

Meanwhile I was falling into a dark pit both physically and spiritually. My eighty-four-year-old mother was slipping away into the world of dementia, and I, an only child, remained her primary caregiver. Living two lives 24/7 is exhausting, and when the other party does nothing but complain about her aches and pains—while you remain silent about your own—your nerves become like slabs of beef hanging from hooks in a meat locker. Then add the problem of being asked the same handful of questions over and over, and there's nowhere to go but down.

Thankfully, after each one of those dreadful days with my mother, I had Babe to come home to. First she would howl her displeasure about being left alone and not getting her dinner at the usual time. But after I had waited on Her Majesty and taken her for a walk, all was forgiven and we would curl up on the bed reading and listening to the classical music station. And if I woke up the next morning knowing I was going to have one of those "AIDS days" rushing from bed to bathroom, Babe was always there to give me a compassionate look that said, "I know, my friend. The world has done its worst, but we're still able to sniff the grass and feel the wind blowing on our backs. We can still hear the beauty of birds chirping in the morning and shoo that annoying cat next door off our fence. We can still snuggle together and crawl under the electric blanket when it's cold. (Remember, I like it set on six.) And then there are all those lovely scraps you mix in with my kibble for dinner, which you usually remember to warm up in the microwave. So with all that, we can't really complain too much, can we?"

And so we pushed on—two battered warriors going into battle day after day, determined not to miss out on any fun that life had to offer.

Inevitably, however, the day came when Babe could battle no longer. I found her one early morning on the kitchen floor near her bowls, which wasn't unusual since they were her most precious possessions. But her food bowl still contained the two biscuits I always put there in case she got the munchies during the night. She was lying on one side, breathing heavily. At that hour—it was still dark outside—I knew the vet's office wouldn't be open, and if this was her time to leave me, I didn't want it to be in a strange environment. I bundled her up and laid her on the pillow on her side of the bed. As I crawled into bed next to her, I hoped that our combined smells would bring her comfort.

The sun was shining when I woke up. I looked over and saw that Babe was still alive and that her breathing had become calmer. I called the vet on his cell phone, and he said he was at his second office in Davis, about an hour and a half's drive away. I carried Babe, still wrapped in the blanket, out to the car and set her on the floor on the passenger side, which was warmer than the seat. It was then that I realized I had fallen asleep while still wearing my clothes from the day before. To hell with smelling fresh, I thought.

As I headed for Davis, thoughts of Babe filled my mind. I recalled all the silly adventures and little dramas we had shared. She had been in my life for 22 months, but it seemed like only a few weeks. Then I was hit by the realization that Christmas was only two weeks away, and I lost my composure. We weren't going to have a second Christmas together. I became angry at God and through my tears I kept asking Him why He couldn't have given my brave little dog one more Christmas with me. I looked down at Babe and saw that her eyes were open. She was staring at me, but this time I couldn't see the words in her eyes. Maybe she was studying my face so that she'd remember what I looked like when she had to eventually pick me out from the crowd after I got to heaven: unshaven, wrinkled clothes, hair askew, tear stains on my glasses and cheeks——oh, that was a picture I wanted her to retain.

It was around ten-thirty when we arrived at the vet's office. He made a wonderful suggestion. "Why don't you take her out to our garden?" he asked. "There's a fountain and pots of poinsettias and the final crop of roses is in bloom. That's a much nicer place to say goodbye than on a metal table under fluorescent lighting. After you've had some time together, I'll come out and we'll say goodbye to her there."

I laid Babe's blanket-wrapped body near the fountain. With the sound of water trickling in the background, I told her how much I loved her and how much I had enjoyed our time together. I also told her that in heaven she'd have four legs again just like all the other dogs. I told her how she had been my hero; how inspired I had been by her tenacity to get on with the business of living despite the obstacles placed in her path; how she had never had any use for self-pity. And finally I said that I'd be joining her in a few years and then we would be able to chase balls and play tug-of-war whenever we wanted.

The vet and an assistant came into the garden and prepared Babe for the end. I looked away when they inserted the needle into her remaining front leg, but a second later I looked back. "She's gone," the vet said almost immediately. Her eyes were open, but they focused on nothing. The assistant removed the needle. Then for the first time since I had known him, I saw tears in the vet's eyes. "It never gets any easier," he explained, "but it's such a privilege to free them from pain."

I was given the option of leaving the body for cremation or taking it back with me. I chose the latter because a local shelter offered a cremation service that included the return of the ashes in a redwood box; I already had three little boxes on the bookshelf in my bedroom. (Maude was buried in the backyard of the house

I owned when she died.) Several days later a fourth box was added to the collection. In a week I would be facing Christmas with no dog dragging ribbon around the room or tearing apart a stocking filled with chew bones and toys.

The holiday was truly the worst I could recall as an adult. Besides not having a Beagle around, I had to endure the presence of my mother sitting on a sofa surrounded by unopened presents that she had no interest in. And to top it off, I had diarrhea all day. Fortunately I had made a breakfast casserole the night before, so all I had to do was put it into the oven to bake while I went back and forth between the living room and the bathroom.

It is now over a month into the new year. After my dogs before Babe had gone, friends always asked me when I was going to get the next one. Now they are asking me if I am going to get another dog. They know that any new dog will very likely outlive me.

I got my first Beagle when I was twenty-five, which means I have been "hounded" for thirty-six years. The thought of finishing my life without another Beagle around to goad me into taking her for walks, harass me because I'm not opening a can of Alpo fast enough, or press twenty toenails into my back while I'm trying to sleep depresses the hell out of me.

Last night, as I lay on my bed, I had an image of Babe lying with me. She was her young, happy self, before the troubles with tumors set in. She was whispering, "You will never find another Beagle as wonderful as I was, but you will find one who will love you as much as I did and who will try to be the best dog she can be. Now go and find her!"

My hero had found a way to guide me, even after her death. And so the quest begins.

· RON NYSWANER ·

KEEPING SAFE AT HOME

Ron Nyswaner likes dogs to be dogs. They guard his property and greet visitors, they run off the deer and keep rabbits out of the garden, they work out their place in the pack and sleep in the barn. Ron does not look on his dogs as substitutes for children. He loves and cares for them, but he does not coddle them. They are dogs.

Nyswaner is a screenwriter with an astonishing resume. He wrote *Smithereens*, *Mrs. Soffel*, the groundbreaking AIDS drama *Philadelphia*, the Peabody Award-winning *Soldier's Girl*, and recently, *The Painted Veil*, starring Naomi Watts and Edward Norton.

Those impressive credentials allowed him to buy a country home in Woodstock, New York, where he became a dog owner. His adventures in the canine world included a badly-behaved dog, a wonderful dog, and many good dogs, but what all the dogs allowed him to see was their steady good nature and their willingness to love and accept him no matter what else was going on in his life.

Quite a lot was going on, not all of it good. Ron details in his memoir, *Blue Days, Black Nights*, that after the huge success of *Philadelphia*, he started on a downhill cycle of drug and alcohol abuse. His addiction took him through the back streets of Los Angeles, New York, and into the arms of a professional hustler, with whom he became obsessed. That relationship ended with a death, whereupon he discovered that nothing that he knew about the hustler was true, even his name.

Ron looked for a lifeline out of his frenetic whirl of addiction and sex, and found it in the stability and resources of the community in which he lived. Part of his salvation came from his dogs, who touched his heart with their enthusiasm and love whenever he returned home, no matter how strung out, embarrassed, or grief-stricken.

His memoir is an unsparing look at drug addiction and male hustlers, in which his small pack of dogs plays a mostly off-stage part. But he was happy to make them center stage during our conversations.

· · · · · · · · · ·

I'VE HAD DOGS my whole life, and the relationships I've had with them have been the most profound—or almost—in my life. I've usually been monogamous, dogwise. There have been times in my life when I've collected as many as three. But right now I'm back to being a one-dog man with my pit bull, Spike.

Reaching way back, there was a dog who was such a strange object of passion. Missy was a little terrier mix inherited from a neighbor, and she was very unpleasant. She huddled under the sofa and would do serious injury to anybody who tried to take her out. She developed a sinus abscess on her face that was constantly running. And yet I loved her very much. I had her all through my teenage years and into college.

When I was in graduate school in New York, I didn't have dogs. Then I moved upstate in 1988, to this rundown, funky house outside of Woodstock. It's a two-story, cream-colored farmhouse built in 1869 on a cul-de-sac at the end of a gravel lane, very long and hidden by trees. There's a big cinderblock barn to one side of it. There's a pear tree, pine trees, an apple tree, and a stream. It's a really lovely spot to raise dogs and to write.

I'm in my office talking to you. There's a bluebird, tapping at my window. He returns every year. This is the first time this year I've seen him. He fights with his reflection in the window.

Within ten days after moving here, I got a Lab puppy. To my partner at the time I admitted that I had given up life in New York City for one reason and one reason only, and that was so I could have a dog.

We'd seen these puppies advertised in the paper, and I swore that we were just going to look at them. But I scooped one up out of the litter, held her in my arms, and took her home. That was Daisy, the first of my country dogs. She was the worst-behaved dog I've ever had. Even worse than Missy, because at least Missy was just huddling under the sofa, growling at people.

Daisy had a very pleasant personality, but she was completely untrainable. We called her Bandit because any time anybody came to work on my house in any capacity, she would jump into their truck and steal a tool. You'd see these furnace-repair guys chasing this dog all over the yard, trying to get a screwdriver out of her mouth. She would let them get within two feet and then take off. One time she managed to get a light bulb in her mouth. I chased her desperately, trying to get it back. Then, in frustration, I had to watch her eat it. She was too quick. I called the vet, but he was calm about it, and he said, "Just watch her carefully."

And nothing happened. She was completely fine, after eating a light bulb.

She was eager to enjoy life, and she entered every day with an almost unbearable enthusiasm. I loved her for that.

Do you remember that Englishwoman who was popular in the eighties? The dog trainer, Barbara Woodhouse? She wrote a book called *No Bad Dogs*. My friends and I used to joke that if she ever met Daisy, she would have to change the title of her book to *One Bad Dog*.

I took Daisy to classes at the YMCA. We'd see these Dobermans and Rottweilers learning all their skills, totally obedient, and here was this very friendly, very loving Lab who just could not sit still. She couldn't sit, she couldn't lie down, she couldn't stay. It was just impossible for her. There was some wiring about training that just wasn't in her brain.

You had to love her lack of conformity. That's the way I've been my entire life. My family, friends, relatives, and high school principals have all said the same thing about me: "Why can't we train him?" Many people probably considered putting a choke collar around my neck. That spirit in me responded to that in Daisy.

I lost her early in her life. She was hit by a car out at the end of the road. I had let her out while I was taking a shower, getting ready to go somewhere. My house is surrounded by sixteen acres of woods and gardens, at the end of a long, long driveway, and usually there's no traffic. I went to look for her, to put her in the house before I left, and I couldn't find her. I walked out to the end of my road with that dreaded feeling—that fear that we have about those things. And there she was.

Right after that I heard about underground electric fences, which I've found to be very effective. I have used them for other dogs.

For a week or so, I didn't want to come home. It's tough when you lose a dog, a dog who has always been there to greet you, who, when you walk in the door, goes completely wild to see you. And she's not there any longer. She's not going to be greeting you. I couldn't bear it.

All my dogs have been free or rescued from the pounds or the streets. So a week later I went to the pound, and found a new dog who cured my grief.

Going to the SPCA is just an excruciating experience if you love dogs. You don't want just one dog to take home, you want to take them all. We walked around, and at the very end of the row, at the back of the cage, there was a shepherd-Lab mix who was just shaking, shaking, shaking. So many of the other dogs were so eager to meet me, barking to be touched. But she was just huddled in the back of the cage. We found out that she had just been dropped off, the last of her litter. All the others had found homes, but they couldn't find a home for this one, so they took her to the pound. She had only been there less than twenty-four hours, which explained why she was so afraid. Of course, that's the one I wanted.

Billie grew into one of the most beautiful dogs I've ever seen. She had the head and body of a shepherd, with the pointy ears, about eighty pounds, lean and trim. She had very thick white fur. She also had some Lab features, so she was extraordinary looking.

I have to say that in many ways Billie was the love of my life. I had to explain it to my fiancé, James, when we met. "By the way, I don't know what's going to happen between us, but I just want you to know there's this dog named Billie in my life, and you'll never take her place." Everyone who came into my life had to understand. Billie was the kind of shepherd-Lab mix that is so eager to be trained and was a perfectly obedient, wonderful dog. You just had to teach her the words a couple times. "Sit." "Stand there, Billie." And she just did whatever you asked.

Soon I gathered another Shepherd mix in my life, a boy. He

was really pathetic. At the pound, he wouldn't even stand up. Totally inexplicably, we named him Chaac, after the Mayan rain god. There was nothing at all about him that resembled a god. He always had his tail turned under and his ears pressed down. He was frightened of life. His mother had the pups in the woods, and he was utterly feral. We had to rehabilitate him. Eventually my friends started calling my house a rehab because I was taking in these dogs who were shaking and traumatized.

I inherited the third dog who became part of that pack. My nephew, Kevin, died of AIDS in 1992. In the last six weeks of his life, he adopted an Akita-shepherd mix. He called her Sadie. She had been hit by a car, and had a broken foot. My sister-in-law, while she was taking care of her son, ended up taking Sadie to the vet twice for foot operations. I thought she was pretty remarkable for doing all that. He asked me if I would take her, and I had refused because I had these two big dogs already. It was hard enough to find people to take care of them when I went away, and there was all that expense when I had to board them.

At Kevin's memorial service, everybody who stood up, even doctors and nurses, said that what Kevin thought about most in the last days of his life was finding a home for Sadie. It was obvious that I was meant to take her. So Sadie flew home with me right from the funeral in Georgia.

We drove right up to our home in Woodstock from the airport. My other two dogs came up, tails wagging, to greet her. We stopped the car, opened the door, and the first thing she did was attack Chaac. Within thirty seconds, there was screaming and blood everywhere. She sent him to the vet with three puncture wounds. Just home from the airport, we got right back in the car and rushed to the emergency vet.

That was how Sadie came into my life. She terrorized every neighborhood dog. I paid several hundred dollars in vet bills to my neighbors over the years because of Sadie. At least she didn't go seeking out dogs at their homes; she only attacked dogs who wandered onto my property. If they happened to make that mistake they tended to end up in the hospital. It was a little scary, and I probably would have thought about putting her down if she had come to me in any other way.

She was tough, and very powerfully built. She had very thick fur, a Chow-like head, and a black spot on her tongue. She was built for hunting, which she did very well. I loved her because she had been my nephew's dog, and she was very loving to people, just not to any other dog or creature. Akitas can be that way.

Since I live in the country, my dogs live mostly outside. They have a warm place in my barn to sleep when they want. They take care of groundhogs and rabbits and those other pesky little creatures that look cute but destroy your garden. They keep deer away from my plants, which is fine with me, because I'm a gardener. I really enjoy seeing dogs who have a purpose in life, as opposed to being just pampered and treated like children, which they aren't. We treat our dogs very much like dogs.

Billie, Sadie, and Chaac formed a pack, and watching it was really fascinating. They had a whole life that I was not part of. They were happy to see me, and I fed them, and they obeyed me, and I was definitely the alpha. But the three of them worked out a relationship that was very complicated.

The white shepherd, Billie, stepped up, since she was the first on the property. She defended Chaac and punished Sadie for any kind of infraction. She established the hierarchy in very specific ways. For example, when I would drive home, I would step out of my car and the three dogs would come over. Sadie would attempt to walk toward me, and Billie would take her by the throat and take her down. It was worked out that Billie and Chaac would walk toward me to greet me, and Sadie would wait.

I would throw the tennis ball for the dogs. But Billie determined that Sadie was not allowed to play ball. If Sadie touched the tennis ball, Billie would punish her severely: teeth to the throat, down to the ground, really tough. If Sadie was sitting somewhere, I could put the tennis ball right in front of her, and she wouldn't touch it. She wouldn't even look at it. Because Billie had made the rule that she was not allowed to play with tennis balls. They didn't need me; they worked it out themselves. Dogs do that.

They lived together for eleven or twelve years. Eventually, as Billie aged, there came a moment when Sadie attacked her and tried to establish her dominance. That's what dogs in the wild would do.

I was in the city on the day it happened, and the dogsitter was here. It was a vicious, brutal attack. Sadie broke Billie's back. Though they had slept together, played together, and ate together, Sadie had all this pent-up frustration, getting Billie back for all those years she couldn't play with the tennis ball. After that, I kept Billie by my side to take care of her. Even though I try to let dogs be dogs, I had to take care of Billie. First Billie died, then Chaac died, and I was left with Sadie.

It really reinforced for me that dominance is what dogs yearn for. Either you assert dominance, or they do. It was great for me to watch, to see how dogs behave when humans aren't trying to interfere too much with what they essentially are.

In June 2003, my fiancé and I were driving near my house, and we saw a pit bull standing in the middle of the road, literally on the double yellow line. I screeched to a stop, got out of the car, and went up to the dog. He had a collar on and looked like he was in good health. I dragged him off the road. By the time I got back into the driver's seat, he was back in the middle of the road again. Just standing there, oddly enough.

It was real pit-bull behavior. He had determined that he was going to stand on that spot in the road. And no one was going to tell him not to. There is a determination in pit bulls that is really strong. So I put him in my car because I didn't want someone else to come around the turn and hit him.

Spike was a beautiful six-month-old puppy. He has a black eye, like Petey from the *Our Gang* television show. He has the floppy ears. He's white with black spots. I went out in the neighborhood, knocked on doors, put up signs, and didn't find anyone who claimed him. I fell completely in love with this dog, but then, of course, the phone rang. With trepidation, I answered. It was somebody saying, "I think you have my dog." I said, "Oh? Well, describe him."

She described him utterly accurately. Obviously it was her dog. Then her husband got on the phone and started talking about what a bad dog Spike was. He said, "He always broke out of his cage."

I asked, "How long do you keep him in a cage?"

He said, "Well, we work sometimes fourteen hours a day." As soon as he said that, I said to myself, I just have to figure out how to get out of this gracefully. They didn't know where I lived.

But it worked out. I said, "I'm in love with your dog. I'll buy him from you."

The guy said, "How much would you pay?"

You can see what a tough negotiator I am. I said, "How much do you want?"

The guy said, "Twenty dollars."

I said, "I'll give you forty."

He told me where to meet him. I kind of thought there would be a confrontation. But when I met him and his wife, he admitted that he was a little embarrassed because he knew he should never have owned a dog. He said, "We know it's not right to keep a dog in a cage fourteen hours a day."

I said, "Well, he'll be really well taken care of." It worked out for everybody.

Sadie didn't attack him at first because he was a puppy. But on the second day, Spike galloped up to her, wanting to play. That was not the way to approach an older, cranky Akita.

I had boots on luckily. I had to rip them apart with a lot of kicking and yelling. But I got them apart. I've broken up a lot of dog fights in my time, but I've never been bitten.

There is a certain validity to fear of pit bulls because they were bred to fight in the pits. But they were trained not to bite their owners. The owners of the dogs had to lean in to break up the fight at a certain point. They would grab their dogs.

Sadie attacked Spike twice after that, very seriously. At one point, my friends were creating all this well-intentioned drama, saying I had to give Spike away or Sadie would kill him. I even made an appointment to drop him off at a kennel. My heart was breaking, though, and I couldn't do it.

So what I did—I'll tell you, but you'll think I'm crazy. They were hanging out in front of house. I went up to the Akita and the pit bull, and I faced them. I said, "This is it. This is my house, and I have the right to make the decisions here. You are going to live together. And you have to start living together right now."

I know I live in Woodstock, but I'm really not the "touchy-feely" type. But I have to say that from that moment they lived in peace with each other. I had seen dogs work these things out before. And I just figured, They'll work it out. And they did.

Spike learned to be submissive to the older female. He learned you don't run toward Sadie, you approach her from the side. That's how dogs show respect—they never make eye contact. And they were good friends until Sadie's death about a year ago. She was about twelve. All my dogs come to me rescued, so we never know their exact ages.

Spike is the single dog in my life right now. He is the least ferocious and fearsome pit bull there is. He is so popular that he should run for mayor of Woodstock. People don't invite me any more, they invite Spike, and I come along. He is fascinated by babies, and he loves my three-year-old goddaughter. I take him to kids' soccer games. He's like a mascot.

I'm very passionate about Spike. But I have to say I'm also very passionate about my fiancé. I should make that clear. James never had a dog in his life—never, not as a child, not as an adult. He's an actor and lived in an apartment in New York City. Spike is his first dog. He's completely enamored with him.

A day in Spike's life is a day many people would like to have. I get up awfully early, around four-thirty or five, to begin work. Spike does not get up. He sleeps in his crate in the kitchen. It's open—he just chooses to sleep there. He watches me make coffee, then stays in his bed until around seven. Then I figure he needs to get up. I have to sometimes drag him by the collar to the door.

He lives inside, as opposed to my other dogs who used to live outside. He really has no interest in an activity that doesn't include a human being. My other dogs would love to go running and hunting. I used to open the door for my other dogs and say, "Go kill something." And they'd bound out, full of energy.

If I don't go with Spike, he has no interest in going outside. We take a walk at seven, the first of several during the day. Right now he's on an arranged walk schedule with a lady who comes three times a week to relieve me a little of the duty. He has play dates, when I take him to play with other dogs.

People call and borrow Spike. The woman who boards Spike when I'm traveling sometimes calls and says, "I have a dog here who needs some play. Could I borrow Spike?" Spike loves it. I could probably rent him and make a living off him. At a certain point, we'll go visit his friend, a black Lab named Jagger. Spike and I will stop and visit with the kids. He rides in the car while I go shopping. At night he heads for his crate, utterly content to be there.

A pit bull's attention span is very short. You can throw a stick for him once or twice. He'll grab the stick very enthusiastically, see a squirrel, and drop the stick. Or he'll decide to chew on a clump of grass. He doesn't have the intensity that Retrievers have.

I think my dogs have helped me spiritually and emotionally. They are always there for me. They're the perfect companions. The pack of dogs were present during the darkest times in my life, when I was really struggling with drug addiction and a lot of grief.

They have seen me at my worst, walking around the house,

whacked out on drugs, very paranoid. And they kept giving me this complete, unconditional love.

I remember very clearly one horrible binge weekend, when for at least twenty-four hours I hadn't fed them. I was just too screwed up. I remember as I was coming off that binge, I felt this incredible guilt that I had forgotten them. And they were so loyal; they were sitting there, waiting for me, as if nothing unusual was happening. Even though their master was locked in the house, covering the windows with sheets, thinking the FBI was after him. There was no judgment. None at all.

It was hard, recovering from my drug addiction. It took a long time. But I had this great place to live, and it became a kind of rehab for me. One of the steps, as part of my spiritual program, was to make amends to those I'd injured. As soon as I heard that, I knew what I had to do. I had been thinking a lot about the dogs, about how grateful I was to them for sticking with me through all the hard times. They never thought I was crazy. They never ran off when I forgot to feed them. So I made amends to the dogs. I apologized to them, and tried from then on to be attentive to their feeding times and the things that they thought were important.

I talk to the dogs all the time. I think a great thing about having dogs is that you can talk to yourself but pretend you are talking to your dogs. I walk around the house all the time talking. But there's a dog present. So I'm not really talking to myself. Or in the car. They have heard all my screenplay ideas first. What's great about dogs is they don't give a shit about screenplays or Hollywood or my pathetic career. All they care about is the squirrel running through the woods.

All these false things we get attached to—dogs don't. They have a great sense of sanity. They know where the center is. That's why I love dogs.

· RANDALL McCORMICK ·

MESSAGE FROM THE HEART

In churches and cathedrals of southern France, there is often a statue of a saint who holds a staff in one hand while a friendly dog leans against his side. This is St. Roche, patron saint of dog trainers. His story is an interesting one. In 1350, he was the son of the wealthy mayor of Montpellier and lived in aristocratic comfort until one summer when Pope Urban V visited from Rome. Roche was transfixed by the pope's devotion to his faith and decided to make a pilgrimage to Rome. God showed his approval by giving him the gift of healing.

On his return journey, Roche entered village after

village where the plague was decimating people. At each village, he tended to the sick, often curing them. But in the village of Piacerna, Roche himself fell sick.

He didn't want the villagers to see his suffering, as he knew they would tend to him and thus reinfect themselves. So he disappeared into a quiet spot in the woods to live out his days. But a dog followed him to his hiding place, and each day the dog appeared carrying a loaf of bread. Roche ate the bread, which gave him sustenance to recover. When he was strong enough, the dog led him back to the home of his master, where Roche found friendship and the means to start over in his life as a healer.

The cessation of the plague in 1439 was attributed to prayers to St. Roche. In recent times, various priests of the Catholic Church have advised their parishioners that against an epidemic like AIDS, prayers to St. Roche are once again in order.

While dogs aren't needed to carry bread to the sick any more, Randall McCormick's story demonstrates the ways in which dogs help us—as comforters and companions, warmers of the body and the soul. He talked with me from his home in Atlanta about the important part dogs have played in his life.

· · · · · · · · · ·

FOR AS FAR back as I can remember, my family always had animals. Cats, fish, birds, frogs, turtles, rabbits, and, of course, dogs. We were a very large family; I'm the last of seven children.

My father was a plasterer for the city of Milwaukee, and when I was seven years old we moved to a one-street subdivision within the city limits. Our house was right on the border, as far out as you could go and still be in Milwaukee. There was a lot of farmland around us. My parents felt that it was a safe place to raise their kids.

My first recollection of a family dog was a Collie named Queenie. She was a beautiful purebred, and my mom thought it would be a great idea to breed her. We were all in favor of it, because we could each imagine ourselves with our own puppy. But when it came time to do it, Queenie bit the male.

Shortly after Queenie died, at age eleven, my sister-in-law Judy came over and said she knew of a great dog for us. The couple who owned her was going to put her to sleep. It never occurred to my mom that there might be some problem with her. She just said, "Sure, we'll take her."

We were all excited to see our new dog. She was a terrier mix with a mottled brown coat. As soon as Judy put her down on the floor, she ran under the kitchen table and wouldn't come out. I crawled down and reached out to pet her, but she backed away. My mother said she spent the whole first night sitting under the table, trembling. She was afraid of everybody and everything. It made us wonder if she had been abused.

My dad put her in a crate, and she whined a lot. He let her out, and my brother Tom fed her treats and talked gently to her, and she bonded with him. She decided he was her human, and she stuck by him. She even slept in bed with him at night.

We named her Taffy. She was not the nicest dog in the world. She never really bit anybody, but she threatened to. She bared her teeth and growled at anybody she didn't know.

A year later Tom got married and moved to his own house. He couldn't take Taffy because she didn't like his wife—or anyone else, for that matter. She decided to be friends with my next brother in line, Mark. But it was the same story with him. He was already eighteen, and two years later he got married and moved out. At that point, Taffy latched onto me. I was the only kid left at home, so she really didn't have any other choice. We both missed my brothers. I was pleased that this funny-looking creature had decided to love me.

I wasn't a lonely child, but I was alone a lot. I had friends, but not a best friend. Taffy became my best friend. She waited at the front door for me to come home from school and followed me through the fields on my walks. At night she jumped up on my bed and snuggled under my arm. I was comforted by the gentle rise of her ribs with each breath and I fell asleep with her nose pressed against my skin.

She had at least four litters of puppies. She was the only female dog on our block, so when she went into heat, it seemed all the males came a-calling. She'd be in the front yard, bumping uglies with my friend John's dog. And nine weeks later, out came the puppies. They were very cute. My mother found homes for them.

To the outside world, she was not the nicest dog, but to me, she was a great love. We had something special. She gave me an experience of something I would never forget, unconditional love.

She came with me when I moved away from home. She was getting older, and she had separation-anxiety issues. She didn't want to be left alone. I had to have her put down when she was seventeen. But she had a great life.

Fast-forward to the year 1984. I was living in Milwaukee, involved in a lot of athletics and playing softball for a gay bar called M&Ms. On Memorial Day, we were playing in the Wreck-Room Classic against twenty-six softball teams from all over the country.

I happened to notice one guy in particular. He had a big bushy mustache and was very handsome. He saw me looking at him, and he shot me a smile that just about melted my heart. He kept on walking, but then he turned around and asked me to dinner. I accepted. I was all of twenty-one at the time and he was thirty-two. That was John Brooke.

He was such a wonderful man. He went back to Atlanta after that weekend, but we kept in touch and visited each other, and pretty soon I was asking my friends whether I should move to Atlanta or not. Everyone said the same thing: "He's too old for you."

I didn't think that at all. I went with my heart. By August, I was living in Atlanta with him.

Naturally we told each other everything, all about our childhoods and former relationship stories. I told him Taffy was my great love, before him.

Our first Christmas together he surprised me; my present was a beautiful Miniature Schnauzer. We named her Foxxy because the man we got her from was named Tom Fox. She was just a ball of fur, but she grew into a beautiful silver and gray dog with a wonderful personality. We bought our home together in the summer of 1986, the same house John had rented for many years. It was a stressful time, but we managed. You know what it takes to ease some of the problems a couple can have? A little of that unconditional love. I hadn't realized it, but my dogs were a good learning experience.

When I moved here to be with John, there was no such thing as safe sex, but in 1985 the first international conference on AIDS was held in Atlanta, so we heard about it all the time on the news: Some 5,600 people died that year of AIDS, including Rock Hudson.

We started to play safe with each other. John decided to get tested for HIV in 1987, but he wasn't sick, so we weren't too nervous. At that point, we still didn't know many people who had it. He came home from the doctor's office and just stared at me with an almost terrified look. He said his life was over as we knew it. He had tested positive.

That news just about crushed us. Any long-term plans we had made as a couple were put on hold. We had to concentrate on the here and now. All my energy went into taking care of John's health.

It took me another year before I went to get tested. I had pretty much psyched myself up for the fact that I was going to be positive. After all, with John sick, I saw the writing on the wall. To my utter shock, when the counselor told me I was negative, I broke down in tears. I told him, "How could that be? My lover is positive. How am I supposed to go home and tell him that I am negative?"

John was so relieved that he had not given it to me that we both cried. He had told me that I could leave—he would not ask me to go through all of what was to come. I told him that I was not in just for the fun of it; we were committed to each other for the long haul. I loved him all the more for being so sensitive to my feelings.

John started to show symptoms in 1989. He had to have a blood transfusion six months after starting AZT. No other drugs had been approved yet, so it was a guessing game for doctors. From the onset, John was on no less than twenty pills a day. He was also involved in studies for new drugs. He thought it might one day lead to the eradication of this horrible disease.

From that time forward, when he was home sick, Foxxy was by his side. She was like his little nurse. She would lie next to him in bed and give him all her attention. It's funny, the way dogs have this sense that something is wrong. It was like she was trying to give him something, as though she knew he had AIDS—she wanted him to fight and come through it.

For five years, John battled this terrible disease. John, Foxxy, and I all battled it together, like a tight little family. But in April 1993, after all his valiant effort, my lover, John P. Brooke, died.

Foxxy and I felt lost. There just seemed no way to repair the huge hole of John's absence. We didn't want to go out of the house or talk to anybody. We couldn't feel good about anything, even grilling a steak or some special thing to eat. I didn't want to go on, but Foxxy was there, and she needed me. Some days the only thing that kept me going was needing to feed her and take her for her walk.

When you lose someone close to you, it never leaves you. I was just thirty years old. That was the worst year of my life. My mother told me that I was way too young to be having this much death in my life.

In 1999, Foxxy was fifteen years old. First she started to have some female problems; then she developed a tumor that became an open sore. The vet told me that, at her age, it was just not treatable. I finally realized that her time was coming very soon.

I really didn't want to let her go. She was the last vestige of John. But she was sick. I could tell that her suffering had become pretty bad.

So I told all my friends that I was going to Florida for a long weekend. On that Friday night I took her to the Humane Society to have her put down. The staff gave me all the time I needed to say my goodbyes. All the pain of losing John came back as I sat in the exam room with her. I stroked her and promised her that she was going to see John in just a few minutes and she could lick and kiss him all she wanted.

When it came right down to it, I just couldn't be in there when she passed. The loss was very profound.

It took me two years before I could think about getting another dog. When I finally got one, I decided it had to be completely different from any dog that I had ever had before. I'd had only small dogs, so I thought a big dog would be nice. That's how I got it in my head to get a Rottweiler.

I named him Caesar. He was very sweet. He would not hurt a flea, but had way too much energy for me. I felt guilty for not spending enough time with him to get rid of that excess energy. The first week I got him, I had to travel on business, so I took him to my friend's house. When I came to pick him up, my friend said, "Never again." Turns out that Caesar had completely ripped up a bathroom, and just before dinner guests arrived, he had crapped all over the house.

None of my friends wanted to take care of him because he was so rambunctious. I was traveling a lot and just didn't have enough time to dedicate to him. I finally realized that it was just not fair for him to be cooped up all the time. I had to put him up for adoption.

Into my life came a very nice woman named Patience. She called and told me she had always had Rotties and she would have nothing but another one. She had a female who was seven years old, but the dog had cancer. Patience wanted another Rottie to ease her other dog's last days. So I invited her to come over and meet Caesar.

I'll never forget that day. A woman with two kids drove Patience to my house. Out of the station wagon came this small woman, about eighty-five years old, with gray hair, five foot two, and using a walker. The kids ran up to me and started playing with Caesar right away. I had to walk him down the drive to Patience because it was too hard for her to walk up. I thought, This won't work—he'll knock her down, and she'll pass on.

But then she told me her story. I had noticed she was kind of bruised and battered. She said a door-to-door salesman had come to her house trying to sell her some pest control for her house. When she said she didn't want that service, he became angry and started yelling at her. Then he took the pesticide and sprayed her in the face. He tried to rob her, but she blocked the way with her walker and started screaming. He ran away. The story was in all the papers. She was in the hospital for quite a long time, and her skin still looked burned. The police caught the guy, and she was suing him and the company he worked for. It was a terrible ordeal for her.

I told her how rambunctious Caesar was, but that didn't bother her. She said she was quite good at dog training, and she had a caregiver living with her to help.

Even though it didn't seem like the best situation for an eight-month-old Rottweiler puppy, there was something about Patience that made me say OK.

So she took Caesar home with her.

Patience calls me all the time to tell me how happy Caesar is. She has a huge yard for him to run in. I went up to see him about six months ago, and he was just as wild as he ever was. He was so happy to see me that he leapt straight up in the air. But he's so careful around Patience. He doesn't knock her over. And there have been no more incidents with angry salesmen! Looking at Caesar with Patience, I felt that I had made the right decision.

By 2005, I was wanting a dog again. This time, though, I was going to look for one that was very sweet, not as big as Caesar, and certainly not as wild. I decided on a Boxer. I looked for about three months. In December, I came across an ad in the paper about a litter of Boxers. I called the people, and they came across as careful, professional breeders.

On a warm Saturday morning, I drove up to Conyers, which is not exactly close. I was invited in and was shocked at how the people lived. No one had cleaned that house in a long time. There was a heavy smell of dogs. There were dishes of food, coffee cups, newspapers, hairpins, wet towels, empty rolls of toilet paper, and hundreds of toys lying all over the floor. There was a two-year-old girl standing in the corner.

The guy looked embarrassed and said, "Let's go around back." The dogs were out in the backyard. His wife came out, and she was kind of disheveled, too.

They told me it was their first litter, which was not the impression they had given over the phone. They had the mother and father on site. She had had a litter of ten. They had six left—two boys and four girls. I wanted a male. I had grown up with female dogs, and Foxxy, of course, and I wanted to switch to a boy. Well, of the two boys, one had mange and was a bit on the smallish side. The other boy came right up to me. They had just put a huge bowl of food down for them to eat. All the puppies were eating ravenously, but this one kept running back and forth from me to the food. I had them take him out of the fenced area. He and I played for about forty-five minutes. He was cute, cuddly, and wanted to be with me, not back with his family.

But the thing that really got me was the small patch of gray just under his lower lip. You see, I've had a goatee for many years.

Until I turned thirty, it had been brown, just like the hair on my head. In the year after John died, my goatee turned gray, just like this puppy's. We looked like each other. Once again, I felt my heart say, "That's the one."

I had to have him. He is a beautiful brindle, just like his daddy, sleek and muscular, with big brown eyes.

Coming home in the truck, he bundled himself up under my jacket and went to sleep. Like he knew he was safe. At home, he was no problem. He trained himself. I never had to yell at him. He hasn't barked yet, except for the time he turned around and saw himself in the bedroom mirror. Scared the piss out of him! He thought another dog had snuck up on him, and he let out a yelp.

Last month, I started to feel a pain in my gut, as if I had eaten something bad, and Samson all of a sudden had to be right with me. I lay down, and he lay down on top of me. I got up, and he was stuck to my side. The pain was getting worse and worse, and finally I had to call Dan to take me to the emergency room. Samson was so worried, but we couldn't peel him off me. It took both of us to get him in his kennel. He knew something was wrong.

We got to the hospital, and they rushed me into surgery. I had a ruptured appendix. It's funny, but Samson knew it—he had a sense that something was wrong, even more than I did. All the dogs I've had have been like that.

Now Samson is about seven months old and thinks he owns the place. He's sweet, loves to cuddle, and is not rambunctious— most of the time. He is content to lie at my feet. He makes me laugh. He lies in bed with me to make sure I am warm and loved. He is carrying on the work of every other dog I have ever had. At forty-three, I think I won't ever be without a dog again. The unconditional love they give is powerful and rich. I just hope I exude that kind of love to him.

MAKING THE WORLD A BETTER PLACE FOR DOGS

TRAVIS

Job Michael Evans, the late, great monk of New Skete dog trainer, used to say that every dog trainer in the world has his secret closet of failures, dogs whom it was simply impossible to train. And anyone who said they didn't was lying.

Evans, who passed away from AIDS in 1995, said that the challenge was what to do about such dogs, because they simply could not be permitted to live in human society. He also said that putting a dog to sleep was not the worst thing that could happen to a dog, that sometimes not euthanizing the dog was worse because then disaster would thrive for the humans and for the dog.

Any dog lover understands that dogs have physical limitations that mean we will most likely outlive them. Though we may not like it, we acknowledge that cancers, infections, organ failure, or the simple fact of old age may one day separate us from our beloved companion. But what if a dog's problems are mental rather than physical? Is there a dog so bad that neither love nor pharmaceuticals can help him? Jay Quinn, the talented author of the novels *Metes and Bounds* and *Back Where He Started*, faced that problem with his "boy dog," Travis.

Jay took full responsibility for Travis. Working with his vet, he did the best he could to train Travis, and then to medicate him when training just wasn't enough. His story is a model for love and sacrifice, as Jay did what a loving owner must to do to protect other dogs, and in the end, to protect Travis as well.

. . . .

NO ONE CAN ever say I didn't want Travis. He was my baby, my buddy. In many ways, he was my alter ego and we glommed onto each other's neuroses like parent and child often do. I found my entire household working to accommodate his moods and his idiosyncrasies with the benevolence sometimes extended to troubled children. I did everything I could for seven years. No one can say I didn't.

I am a dog person. I've always had dogs, and I would have dogs as part of my new home with my partner. I wanted a pair of yellow Labs. However, purebred dogs would have set me back far more than my budget at the time would have allowed. Instead I combed the pet section of the classified ads for mixed-bred puppies that were close to the loving nature of Labs.

An ad appeared one Saturday in February for puppies that were half yellow Lab and half red Doberman Pinscher. The pups were waiting for adoption at a pet-rescue facility run by a veterinarian way up on the western side of Boca Raton. I called and told them to hold onto any males they had, I was on my way up.

I got a newspaper-recycle bin small enough to fit in the cab of the pickup and lined it with shredded newspapers. I knew the pups would probably get motion-sick or piddle as a result of riding in the truck on the way home. I was well prepared in that event, and in others as well. I had already gone to the pet superstore and bought metal bowls for food and water. There were two new kennels, waiting to be set up. I'd also bought teal-colored leashes and collars.

On the forty-five minute drive I thought about the mix of Doberman Pinscher and Labrador Retriever. I had friends with red Dobies, and they were wonderful animals—very protective, very loyal. I knew yellow Labs to be mellow and playful. I had myself convinced the two breeds would cancel out any negative qualities of the other and make for wonderful pets. Lab and Dobie: What would I tell people they were? Labermans? Dobadors sounder better. Dobadors it would be.

I already had names picked out. At the time, I was working for a land-surveying company. On the days I spent in the office drafting or marking up site plans to show utility locations, I listened to the local country station, KISS-FM. That total immersion in country music had leaked into my choice of radio stations in the truck and at home. My partner liked Randy Travis and I liked Travis Tritt, so "Randy" and "Travis" were ready to be claimed by the pups.

When I got to the pet-rescue place, a vet assistant took me to the outdoor kennels, explaining that all the male dogs but the runt had been adopted already and urged me to pick one of the females, agreeing that the two dogs would keep each other company while my partner and I were at work.

My heart broke when I saw them. They were living on the concrete floor of a kennel that wasn't exactly clean. They were skinny as all hell. You aren't supposed to be able to count a puppy's ribs. I could count every one. The vet assistant told me the owners of the pups' mama had dumped them there when they were only five weeks old. The dam was a purebred red Dobie, and they had planned to breed her and sell the pups. However, a neighbor's yellow Lab had gotten to her first, and disgusted, they'd wanted nothing to do with the bastardized offspring. She assured me that all they needed was a good home and they'd fatten right up. More fool, me.

I picked up the scrawny runt and held him against my chest. He was auburn colored and bony, with the broad brow and square head of a Lab. He nuzzled me and whined pitifully. I rubbed the back of his head gently with one finger and he sighed, laid his head on my forearm, and closed his eyes contentedly. The runty boy dog was going home with me.

I looked down to the shrill yips of a female who went defiantly for my sneaker lace. She gripped it in her teeth and tugged mightily as if to tell me to put her brother down, right now. I squatted with her brother resting on my arm and picked her up gently under her belly. Standing, I shifted her awkwardly to rest on my other arm, where she promptly bit me.

"Well, you little hussy," I fumed. She was much more of a Dobie than her brother. She had the long nose and slender head. Similarly colored, the little girl pup had fantastic tawny eyes, more gold than brown, more yellow than green, not unlike my own. She resisted being held and instead struggled to my other arm to lay on top of her brother, who did little to object. "I'll take them both home," I told the vet's assistant.

Inside, doing the paperwork, they asked me what I was going to name them. I didn't hesitate telling them the boy dog would be Travis, but I had to think quickly to come up with a name for the girl dog. I looked at her. My partner liked Patsy Cline, and by her coloring and feistiness, she reminded my of a neighbor lady I had while growing up. Her name was Patsy as well. So Patsy she became.

The pups were not easy to love. They were horrible little rat dogs with sharp teeth and mean natures. Patsy never missed an opportunity to be mean to her brother. She wouldn't let him eat. She wouldn't let him cuddle. She wanted him dead, it seemed. I kept warning her that she'd better play nice. One day he'd be bigger than she was. Of course, she paid no attention. I had to protect the boy dog from her aggressiveness. So, from the get-go, Travis grew partial to me. As is often the case, two dogs in one home will bond with separate people in the family. Patsy bonded with my partner and became overbearingly spoiled as a result. As if Travis wasn't spoiled to the point of utter obnoxiousness also.

At night, they would finally settle down as we read or watched television. Patsy slept on my partner's chest, her long Dobie nose stretched upward to rest on his neck, under his chin. Travis curled contentedly by my side, like a doggie donut, my hand gently stroking his head or curled protectively along his side. Of course, those were the moments of peace in an otherwise vicious cycle of fighting and looting. My pups were incorrigible, and I was no better than a permissive parent bewildered by a psychotic child. I always said God knew what he was doing making me queer. If my dogs were anything to go by, I'd spend my days in juvenile hall if I had human children.

Patsy became somewhat civilized as she grew, but Travis grew only meaner. He broke into my neighbor's house by charging through her sliding glass door's screen. I found it impossible to walk him at the same time as his sister. When they weren't attacking each other, they were attacking passersby on the narrow sidewalk that surrounded the development where we all lived in West Broward County.

I should have known he was going to be constant trouble when an older lady Travis and I passed each morning took to carrying a substantial umbrella for protection. She didn't speak English, and I didn't speak Spanish. Travis spoke only paroxysms of vicious barking and baring of teeth. I would have to pull him bodily off the sidewalk to let her pass.

I tried every training trick I knew to curb his overprotectiveness. While Patsy responded very well, Travis did not respond at all. If anything, his resolve and single-minded responsibility to protect me was only enhanced by aversion training, behavior modification and the hatefulness of a shock collar. Travis literally tried to kill anyone or anything that came near me. He grew to become ninety pounds of muscley, seething anger and menace. He could launch himself airborne at skateboarders, bicyclists, elderly people with canes, cars; motorcycles in particular freaked him out.

As bad as he was, only I could control him. In his absolute frenzy of aggressiveness, somewhere there was the baby boy dog he reverted to each night, curling himself next to me on the sofa and sighing in relaxation and contentment.

Over the years, Travis came to dominate the house. He attacked my partner, whom the vet said Travis considered subordinate in the pack. He began to bite people. He grew so agitated that he would demand to go outside and patrol the front of our house many times every night.

My vet is a good man who owns and trains Dobermans. But even for him, Travis was a mystery. Over the years, Travis was on acepromazine, an animal tranquilizer; then Xanax and Elavil. The drugs would work for a while, then they wouldn't. Travis was some piece of work.

When he and Patsy were five, my partner and I were asked to adopt a two-year-old female Weimaraner from friends who could no longer keep her. They knew how dog crazy I was, and they also knew that I would give her a home where dogs got every bit of the love and care straight people reserve for their children. So Hailey the Weimaraner came to live with us.

I won't tell you the first weeks were easy. I had to be on constant surveillance to keep Travis from attacking her. I would not have the sweet-natured Hailey tormented by Travis. For the first time in his life, Travis found himself severely disciplined for his overt acts of terrorism. No dog in my house is allowed to run roughshod over another. I could always rationalize away Travis's meanness to humans, but never to another defenseless animal.

Travis settled down and grudgingly allowed Hailey a place in our home. Eventually she became his running buddy, his partner in crime. I watched as the Weimaraner developed separate relationships with both Travis and Patsy. Like a youngest child, she found her place, stood her ground, and integrated herself seamlessly into the pack. I made extra time for her, for Travis, and for Patsy, giving each special, separate attentions. I began to understand my mother more, because she had had three small children at the same time. One is always crying, one is always needy, and one is always swinging from a chandelier in glee.

As with many dysfunctional households, my dog children were very well behaved once you made it into the house. Unfortunately, all the peace in the house lasted only as long as Travis's mind was under control. In fall 2003, my boy dog's mental state started collapsing. In October, he attacked Patsy, his sister, so badly one Sunday morning that she had to be rushed to the emergency vet for staples on her nose. Both my partner and I were coming to the end of our patience. Travis was disrupting our entire household as it bent to attempt to anticipate his sudden bouts of craziness.

I took him to the vet and asked what we could do, short of putting him down. Nearing a last resort, he said we'd try phenobarbital to try and break the cycle.

Walking him in front of the house one afternoon after work, a little boy about ten years old came out of nowhere on a skateboard. Travis went insane. Travis always wore a heavy-duty training collar called a "pinch collar" due to their teeth that form a tight unpleasant grip around a dog's throat when they are tugged or if they lunge. The links on Travis's pinch collar were two inches long, with inch-and-a-half "teeth." He broke it going after the little boy on the skateboard.

"Kid! Freeze!" I shouted. "Don't look at him. For God's sakes, don't look him in the eye." The kid kicked off his skateboard and froze in place.

"Travis!" I shouted. "Sit!"

Miraculously, Travis stopped in midstride of a dead run and sat. I managed to get to him and reattach his pinch collar. He looked at the little boy, not twenty feet away and growled, showing his teeth.

"Kid, he's scared of your skateboard. Please don't move until I can get him back in my yard. Please."

The little boy just looked at me. I managed to pull and drag a snarling, whiny Travis back into my yard. He turned on me, then, whipping around and snapping at me. I pulled his collar straight up in an effort to get him to sit on his haunches; instead, he leapt up with the tug. Frightened now, I stopped and relaxed the pull on his leash. "It's OK, baby. The bad thing's gone. Shhhh, it's OK." Travis relaxed enough to allow me to drag him into the house.

This was when he was on phenobarbital.

At Christmas, Travis attacked my friend Joe and bit me when I put myself between them.

During January, Travis settled down some. He still could be infuriated by passersby to the point that we always had to keep the shutters on the street-facing windows closed. He tried to go after boats on the canal, which particularly infuriated him. But the medicine seemed to calm him.

Then, in early February, Travis lost it on two consecutive nights, attacking the other dogs for no reason.

The second time I pulled him off Hailey, he'd gashed her snout as he had Patsy's. Something in me snapped. Calmly, I looked at him and he looked back at me. I think now some form of communication passed between us. I hate people who imbue their dogs with cuddly human characteristics. Dogs communicate but they don't talk. Still, in that looking into each other's eyes, I feel like Travis and I held a simple two-way communication:

"I can't take this any more, Travis."

"Then, do what you gotta do. I don't care."

I got Travis and Patsy both into their kennels. I had wound care solution on hand, and I doctored Hailey's gash. Though the skin was torn, the muscle below was intact, and I knew it would heal on its own if I kept the wound clean. I allowed her to settle herself on the sofa, stunned and needing some quiet time.

I went into the kitchen and called my partner to tell him the time had come to do the unthinkable. Fortunately, he was out of town on business; I've always found it easier to do the impossible on my own. Once, in severe chest pain, I got up out of our bed in the middle of the night and drove myself to the emergency room. Taking Travis to die would be something I had to face on my own.

On the way to work the next morning, I stopped by the vet's office and told them what happened. I also told them it was time. Sympathetically, they told me to bring Travis in at five o'clock. They told me I didn't have to stay. They could take care of him for me. I told them no. This was part of the responsibility of having a pet. I had to walk the last little way with him.

All nobility aside, I told them I'd need some tranquilizers for Travis, strong ones, just to be able to get him calm enough to get into the car. I told them I'd stop by on my way home from work in the early afternoon. If they'd have the bill and the pills ready for me, I'd appreciate it.

I could barely concentrate the rest of the morning at work. When I finally could leave, I drove straight to the vet's, picking up the pills and paying the bill ahead of the appointment. I knew if I didn't, I'd never make it back.

At home, I took each of the dogs out for a walk separately and then returned them to their kennels, which was unusual but not unheard of. I waited until nearly four to give Travis a staggering dose of acepromazine, and then I spent an agonizing hour waiting for it to take effect.

It never really did. I still had to get a muzzle on him and

needed my neighbor's help to get him in the car. He snapped at us twice before we were on our way.

Travis was pretty quiet on the drive to the vet's office. I took a roundabout route, knowing I'd never be able to drive the same way again. Travis enjoyed the ride quietly, often looking at me with a happy, panting smile as if he was reassuring me.

When we got to the vet, they ushered us into an examining room, and we sat waiting while all the other appointments wrapped up. The tranquilizers hadn't even made Travis sleepy or stumbly. He sat stoically by my side, with an eye on either door so no one could slip in on us unawares. He had a solemn guard-dog stance. I used to call him Lance Corporal Travis because he had the expressionless menace of a Marine on guard duty when he was sitting next to me. I stroked his head and down his back while we waited.

I didn't know my vet had the day off, so I was surprised to see a young woman in a white coat come into the room. She introduced herself and told me that in twelve years of practice, she had only had to put down one dog for being vicious. She asked me if I had thought of any other options, and if I was sure I wanted to do this.

I told her that people used to stop me on the street, Spanish guys usually, and admire Travis. I couldn't make out much more than them asking me if he could fight. They still fight dogs, illicitly, down in Hialeah and the boondocks of Dade County. I was terrified that if I put an ad in the paper or gave him to the animal shelter, someone would adopt him just to fight him. Travis was ninety pounds of solid muscle, but I knew him as my sweet boy who would lie next to me with deep sighs of contentment on the peaceful evenings. I couldn't let him get into a ring with pit bulls. They'd throw him in the ring just for sport, just to whet the pit bulls' appetite for blood. I told her I'd shoot him myself before I'd do that to him.

She nodded and gently asked me if I didn't know of somewhere, somebody, with a lot of land, maybe a farm, where Travis would be the only dog

I asked her how I could give him to someone knowing he might harm a child? What would they do to him? Would they beat him? Would they teach him to be meaner than he already was? How could I give him to somebody who wouldn't care for him the way I had? How could I do that?

She nodded and put his file on the counter, telling me that she had read his entire folder. She didn't know of any way we could have done better by him, other than keeping him so doped up that he would have no quality of life.

Travis paced nervously, ignoring her, ignoring me. She asked me if I'd given him the acepromazine. I told her that I had, and when I had.

She nodded. "I can see that it hasn't even relaxed him." Her voice then took on a direct, comforting tone. "I don't want this to be any worse than it's going to be already. I don't want him to fight. What I'm going to do is to give him a heavy dose of a muscle relaxer. That way, it won't be ugly."

I nodded. She gave me the best reassuring smile that she could muster. I felt sorry for her. Animal doctors are just like people doctors. They are trained to make animals well. They hate to help them die unless there is no other possible way.

In a moment, a vet tech returned with her. Together, they held Travis and gave him the shot of the muscle relaxer in his neck. "It won't be long. I'm going to leave you with him for a few minutes so he feels secure. Then I'll come back and give him the shot. OK?"

I nodded once more. Having made the decision, there was only mute acknowledgment and acquiescence I slid off the bench by the wall to sit cross-legged on the floor, eye level with my boy.

Travis escorted the vet to the door and then turned to walk around, suddenly disoriented. He came to stand in front of me, and his head swayed as if he was following the room as it started to spin. He spread his front legs broadly to brace himself on the rolling deck the floor under us had become. It was only then that he looked at me as if to plead for help. I whispered to him comfortingly and patted his rump gently to let him know he could sit. Helplessly, he sank to his haunches, but he did his best to resist the medicine. Finally he began to sink as his front legs moved away from him. I scooted forward so his head would lie on my lap as he gave in.

Once he allowed himself to sink into my lap, he sighed and closed his eyes. I rubbed his big ol' head and sang a little to him. I always sang a little to him, you know? When he was sweet and calm and happy, I'd find a chorus of "Sweet Thing" or "Gonna Take a Miracle" or "There Is a Rose in Spanish Harlem" somewhere in the back of my memory. When he'd given up the hard day's work of looking after me and simply lie safe next to me on the sofa, curled up like a puppy, I'd sing low and growly to let him know everything was all OK. He'd yawn and stretch out those long Dobie legs and look up at me with dark brown eyes as if to say, "Everything is OK, isn't it?"

The doctor returned with the syringe. She knelt by us and warned me it wouldn't be quick. "Travis is a big dog. He won't go fast. I'm just telling you so you'll be prepared, OK?" With that, she found a vein in his front leg and gave him the shot.

When she had finished, she knelt beside us to wait. I leaned his big head over onto my lap and hummed because I was way past singing. I leaned over him to protect him from all that had bothered him so. And I crooned to him as the last of the fight and life went out of him. It seemed to last forever, but since I had brought him to this place, there was no way I could let him go any further without him knowing I was with him, and everything was going to be OK.

After nearly five minutes, the doctor checked her watch, placed the stethoscope over his heart and listened. "He's gone," she told me.

I don't cry easy, and I don't cry often. What gets torn from me when I do is ugly and harsh and private. Lifelong smoker's sobs aren't pretty. They are hoarse and tearing and hurt to hear as much as they hurt to let go. You could pull concrete from my chest, and it couldn't sound any worse. Practiced hardness doesn't let go easy. What it holds back, the gravel of grief and the thick choking flood of self-hatred, sounds like hell breaking over a quiet room. Given permission to escape, every grief over every torn nerve and violated scar follows behind.

The doctor laid her arm across my shoulder.

"Why is it so hard?" I managed to say. "Why is it all so goddamned hard?"

She couldn't know I meant living. She couldn't know I meant loving. She couldn't know at all what I meant.

Finally, I took Travis's head in my hands and shifted away so I could put it gently down on the floor. I stood, thanked the vet, and made my way on home.

The following Tuesday, I had to pick up Travis's ashes. I'd paid to have him cremated individually. The box was cardboard with an agreeable wood grain print laminated on the lid. He was heavy, my Travis; he made a lot of ashes. I put the box on the passenger seat and tried very hard not to think about his ride to the vet's. I only thought, Now I am bringing him home.

In life, when Travis was outside his kennel and I was in the bedroom, he lay right by my side of the bed. Sometimes he would move away only as far as the sliding glass doors, where he kept watch for the evil and threats only he could see. I wrapped my own tattered sleep around me more tightly knowing the dog was keeping guard over me.

When I got home, I took the box holding his ashes and put it in the drawer of the bedside table next to my side of the bed. "You're home now, baby. You're back where you can take care of me."

Laying down on the bed, the two girl dogs jumped up to be with me. Hailey fit herself into the curve of my legs. Patsy turned and snuggled herself onto my partner's pillow. Travis rested in the drawer next to us. In the years that have passed since then, Travis has remained part of that tableaux. Still, I have caught glimpses of Travis out of the corner of my eye, panting and smiling, all around the house. My canine Marine sentry, Travis, my crazy boy dog, is never too far from my side, keeping watch to this day.

· RANDY ALLGAIER ·

THE BEAGLE'S GIFT

Can one man make a difference in this world? It's easy to be overwhelmed by the world's problems and feel there is nothing you can do. But that is not Randy Allgaier's approach. He was dedicated to a life of service to community and country long before he acquired a dog, but his Beagle, Darwin, opened up a new path by which to help others.

Randy helped prevent the spread of HIV by getting the California legislature to decriminalize needle exchange. As Randy says, the cost of one syringe is a penny, but the cost of AIDS is millions of dollars and endless suffering.

Randy tested positive twenty years ago and developed AIDS eight years ago. He took the deep pain into which he was plunged and used it as a sword to protect others. He had harbored a secret desire for a dog for many years during his public life, but he knew that a dog would need an owner who wasn't forever flying off to Washington or Sacramento. But eventually the time was right for Randy and his partner, Lee, to adopt a puppy. Randy thought that he knew what the simple joy of owning a dog would be like. But he was wrong. It turned out to be much richer and more surprising than anything he had imagined.

· · · · · · · · · ·

I GUESS MY love of dogs began at conception. If you look in the baby book that my mother kept, my first steps were made trying to catch a neighbor's dog, Tippy, a Cocker Spaniel mix. The entry reads, "Randy loves Peg's dog Tippy."

As a kid, I begged my parents to allow me to have a dog and we had a few, but not for long, because my mother, who made Joan Crawford's obsession with cleanliness seem low-key, couldn't put up with the mess, so we would end up finding a new home for each one.

Each dog wasn't just somebody I loved and adored, but somebody who offered me refuge. One of the things that attracted me to having a dog is the experience of having a good friend. I never had a good close friend as a kid. Partly because I was gay and knew it, or at least knew I was different. But partly also because I went to a private school an hour away from where I lived. The bus would take me home, and I was isolated. Later I went to boarding school.

After college, graduate school and a time in New York City, I moved to San Francisco, where I met my partner, Lee, in July 1988. I was involved with the gay community and joined an organization called Shanti, which provides support for people with HIV. Shanti put volunteers through forty hours of very intense training. Lee was one of the facilitators, and we started seeing each other as friends. Then our relationship grew.

Lee's HIV status is negative. He grew up with dogs on a farm in Tennessee. He had a little Chihuahua named Peanut that he talked about a lot. But maybe because he was allowed to have dogs as a kid, he wasn't as obsessed as I was. Every dog I saw, I would stop and talk to it.

We live in the Castro district. There is a playground and ball field a few blocks away that at the time was like a dog park. When I came home from work, there were all these people out in this ball field with their dogs. The dog people were acting like they were at a cocktail party while their dogs were playing. What attracted my attention was all these dogs playing together, big dogs hanging with little dogs who didn't seem to know they were little playing with Great Danes.

As our tenth anniversary approached, Lee and I decided it was time to get a dog, and we started to research breeds. We didn't want to go the rescue route. I wanted to know the temperament of the dog. We began with these cute Jack Russells we saw everywhere. It took us about twenty seconds to realize that no way could we live with that breed. We also considered the PBGV, Petit Basset Griffon Vendeen, but we heard that they tore things up in people's homes.

I thought back to my childhood, and how I adored my grandmother's Beagle, Brownie. I couldn't get enough of playing with that dog. I remember spending a couple of days at my grandparents' house, sleeping with Brownie, hugging and cuddling. I remember that sweet dog smell. We were the classic "little boy and his dog."

I said to Lee, "What about a Beagle?" We did some research on Beagles, and as far as we could tell, the temperament seemed perfect for us, more laid-back than playful. We started thinking of a name, but we didn't want something cutesy. Every other Beagle we met was named Lucy or Snoopy. The name that popped into my head was Darwin. Charles Darwin had done his research in the Galapagos Islands on the HMS *Beagle*. I thought that would be an interesting play on words.

Since we were taking the month of September off to celebrate our anniversary, we decided it would be the ideal time to acclimate a dog to our household. We looked for breeders in the area and found one who told us about a beautiful red and white boy. I said, "We'll be there this weekend." We traveled with our best friend, Karen, to Napa. We got out of the car, and the breeder came to the door carrying this adorable little red and white Beagle puppy. And the first words out of her mouth were, "Oh my God, you all have red hair!"

At that point the puppy was a little over three months old. He was tearing all over the breeder's house, peeing on the floor, bouncing off walls. Everything that would be a horror to me normally.

Before we left, the breeder told us, "If at any time in his entire life you need to place him, you can bring him back to me." That was a wonderful testament to the kind of person she is. She said she bred not only for conformation but for temperament. We were very enamored of her.

Our puppy was renamed on his registry as Shilagae's Darwin's Equality, which brought our activism into his name. We brought him home, and he immediately peed in the house.

He was actually housebroken very quickly. When he was young, we wouldn't allow him out of the kitchen. We had a child gate to keep him in there, but he learned to jump over it very quickly. He was a good jumper, and he found ways to get out, believe me. He was a very curious little guy. He was always trying to get behind our television, and he broke a VCR. But things that would normally make me crazy didn't matter to me any more. Once he got into our pantry and got a sack of flour. I came home, stared into the kitchen, and all I could see was white. It took me a second to realize it was covered with flour. He had peed into it, too. Pee in the flour, flour all over the place, his pawprints all over the kitchen in white. But because it was Darwin, I didn't turn into my mother and say, "You have to leave!"

Lee was really good about cleaning up after Darwin's flour party. I was pissed. But through living with Lee and Darwin, I've learned to let go of a lot of stuff.

When you say "Bad dog!" to Darwin, he immediately goes under the bed. He doesn't like to be around anger at all. If I'm at the computer writing and say, "Goddamit!" loudly, he'll get up and look at me, very worried. He's very sensitive.

At the time, AOL had a "Beagle Board" where people could post online. I started to interact with other Beagle owners. I got a lot of good advice from a few people who would always respond to my posts. I started to call them the Beagle Moms.

In March 1999, my HIV changed to AIDS, with the diagnosis of pneumocystis pneumonia. At the time, I was working like crazy, running back and forth to Washington. I was on the board of the Human Rights Campaign and starting a statewide advocacy group for LGBT people called CAPE. I was stressing myself to the max. And in six months my health went from being good to just about dying.

I was hospitalized for a week. Lee got the nurses to allow Darwin to come and see me. When I saw him, I cried. He, of course, was only interested in sniffing around the hospital. In true Beagle fashion, he said, "This is a new place—I want to explore it." But when I got home, he didn't leave my side.

I recuperated at home for a month before I went back to work. Darwin was with me the entire time. Lee was bedraggled. He was taking care of me, and he had his work with developmentally disabled adults, which is stressful. So when he would come home and take Darwin out for a walk, it was his saving grace, his time alone. Darwin took care of both of us in a way.

Darwin has an uncanny knack of knowing when I'm sick. He is a creature of habit, but he alters his habit to lay in bed with me all day long. He has this look in his eyes that feels like he knows. It's like he says, "I'm here with you."

The jobs in my career have been very intense. I seem to work best under pressure. If there were deadlines and things were fast paced, doing stuff at federal, state and local levels, flying back and forth to Washington and Sacramento—I loved it. There was a lot on the line because we were trying to make a difference for people. Most of my colleagues were ten years younger than I was. They had a lot more energy. I kept up, but it took a toll on my health. Stress and HIV are not a good mix.

I retired in March 2000. Leading up to retirement, though, was horrible. Like many people, I define myself by my job. I was a wreck about the idea. It was a bigger loss than anything I had experienced. Bigger than any death. And it was a decision that I was making, not a loss that was happening to me.

In a weird way, the support that Lee and Darwin gave me was: They left me alone. That's what I needed. Nobody in my immediate sphere of close friends had been through anything like that. I was forty years old, and I was retiring because of bad health. I didn't want any support from anybody. I wanted to find it in myself.

I made an agreement with Lee that for six months I would do nothing but take care of myself. During those six months, we went to a fundraiser for PAWS—Pets Are Wonderful Support— called Petchitecture. Very prominent local architects and designers build an array of habitats for dogs. They are on display and then up for auction. People are very generous because they have such a good time.

I was so impressed by the organization. They keep people with HIV together with their pets because animals are such a good source of companionship, love and support when people are ill. This allowed low-income people with HIV to get food for their animals. Volunteers come in and walk dogs, do cat-litter maintenance. Having had the experience of Darwin when I was very sick, their mission spoke to my heart in ways that were very important.

It was a small organization, but this fundraiser was huge. They put it on themselves, and I was impressed by that, too. So the day after my six-month agreement with Lee was over, I wrote a letter to their board president and their executive director, explaining my background and my resume. A month later I was on their board, and four months later I was the president, which I was for four years. During that time, we got their budget doubled. They were able to expand their mission to cover people with other disabilities and start an elderly program.

I did aggressive fund-raising. It was a grass-roots storefront organization, and my goal was to make it more professional. I recruited board members who had experience in business. Then I left. I feel that organizations need new board members on a regular basis because it helps to keep things innovative.

Darwin is a key reason I was involved with PAWS. It was a passion about their mission that had me so driven and motivated. I got it at the most basic level. PAWS was seen as a warm and fuzzy, expendable thing, but we were trying to tell people, "We are not expendable. This is an important mission."

PAWS also has a program for the homeless. A group of veterinarians reach out to these folks and make sure their dogs are cared for well and, ideally, spayed and neutered. A lot of homeless people do not want to spay and neuter their dogs. There is so little in their life they have control over. But if you gently work with them, they'll do it.

When Darwin turned two, we wanted to have a party for him. We'd been to other people's parties for their dogs, and it seemed that everything at the event was focused on the people. One thing Darwin really would enjoy would be playing together with a bunch of other Beagles. Darwin recognizes other Beagles, and they have their own way of playing. They love to chase one another, though they don't do as much wrestling as other breeds do. On the AOL Beagle Board, we'd heard about Beaglefests held around the country. There was nothing like that happening here in Northern California. So we wondered, Why not put a Beaglefest together ourselves?

Before we did it, we checked out places where we could have it. Beagles are notorious escape artists. They just follow their nose, and they're gone in two seconds. Everything is focused on the scent.

We decided to send out postings that we would have this Beaglefest in Sausalito. We made homemade dog treats for the dogs and a birthday cake for people that read "Happy Birthday, Darwin." A few people responded, so we knew we would have guests, but we had no idea how many.

When we arrived, on a Saturday morning, there were lots of people playing with their dogs at the park. Then one Beagle came, and then two. Suddenly, lots of other Beagles started coming in, and as the Beagles began to arrive, the other dogs started leaving, until it was a Beagle-only park.

Other than Darwin's breeder, and one of Darwin's playmates from the same kennel, Lee and I didn't know a soul. In all, forty-seven Beagles showed up. And had a great time. Over the years, attendance has grown to around 200.

An amazing group of people come to the Beaglefests. You have African-American, Asian, and white, straight and gay, liberals and people who come from very conservative areas in the state, and none of that matters.

We don't ask for any money. For us, it's a labor of love. We have various contests that only Beagle people would understand: "Longest Ears," "Best Owner/Dog Look-Alike," "Most Obstinate," "Does Not Come When Called," and "Turns Around and Goes in the Other Direction When Called"—all things that are very particular to Beagles.

Some owners take the contests very seriously. We judge the categories by applause. One year, we were doing a Halloween theme and had a great costume contest. Some people had their kids dressed up with their dogs.

I adore watching the littlest of the kids. They are just gleeful, watching all these dogs play. We put nametags on so we can get to know each other. But we all know the dogs' names better than the people's names, so somebody started putting the dogs' names on, like, "Randy, Darwin's Dad." The kids were writing, "Bobby, Bagel's Brother."

We wanted to do something charitable with all these Beagle people. That's in our blood. So we starting accepting donations for California Beagle Rescue. PAWS sponsors a 5-K Walkathon, and I sent a mass e-mail out to all the Beagle people, saying, "Let's form 'Team Beagle,' and walk together." We ended up raising $7,000 for PAWS.

It amazes me how people can have this connection with their dogs through their heart, and all this other stuff doesn't matter. The same was true with the Beagle Moms, those women I met online when we first got Darwin. They were very sweet. They knew I was gay and had AIDS. A group of them had decided to meet in Las Vegas one year, and they invited us to come. They were a lot of fun. We all told stories about our dogs. The first night was cathartic because we were talking about our dogs who had died. Some were talking about Beagles that they rescued and the awful lives these dogs had had beforehand. I talked about how Darwin was such an important part of my life because of my being sick. These women and I connected, and they're still very good friends of mine.

The first year I was on the PAWS board, the Beagle Moms came out for Petchitecture, from all over the country. They are not used to hanging around with gay men. One is a born-again Christian from Texas. Another is a rock-ribbed Republican from Chicago. We talk politics occasionally. But you know, we agree to disagree.

By and large, our connection is through dogs. I never thought that, being a liberal gay guy, I could have people as friends who I really disagree with politically. It taught me this lesson—that I can. Those things, while important to me, are not the essential part of me. I was very touched by that, in ways that I can't quite explain.

My health varies. I had a really bad downfall in December. My meds basically stopped working. I had been going around teaching about Medicare Part D and how that works for people with HIV. I wanted to get this information out because it was important. I was so impassioned and doing so much that I didn't listen to my body and was getting sick again. My T cells, which should usually be around 500, went down to twenty-six. My viral load, which usually ranges between 1,000 and 10,000, moved to half a million. And I developed a case of pneumonia and was weak. I was scared. I didn't know what was going on. My doctor said, "Don't ever do that to me again. You scared the hell out of me."

Now I'm fine. Just ninety days ago, I thought I was going to die. But we changed my meds, and I stayed in bed.

Another wonderful thing Darwin has brought me: My dad and I have a good relationship. But we're WASP men. We don't emote a lot. When I was home recuperating, I got a gift basket from my father. He had cherry-picked what was in it. And one of things was a box of Milkbones. I broke down and cried like a little kid because it showed me that my dad knew me. He understood what was important to me in a way that I had never quite known. That was a turning point in my relationship with my father.

Darwin is in every part of my life. At the Beaglefest we had last October, my father was here for his seventieth birthday. If I had to sum up what Darwin has done in my life, he has allowed me to look beyond all the other things and to see that what really connects people is what is in their hearts. In a sense he's been a conduit—he's like my Buddha. He allows me a very direct connection to somebody's heart. Despite all those things that differ in us, there is something that connects all of us, regardless of politics, sexual orientation or anything else, and he's allowed me to find that. That's an incredible gift.

· DAVID MIZEJEWSKI ·

THE DOGS IN
MY OWN BACKYARD

David Mizejewski is a man on mission. As man-

ager of the National Wildlife Federation's Backyard

Wildlife Habitat program, he works to show people

how their own outdoor area, whether it's a yard or a
balcony, can harmonize with birds, butterflies, and other
wild creatures. David says, "Ecological issues tend to be
overwhelming. There's nothing one person can do about
global warming. But one person can make a difference in
their own home, by making it a better spot for wildlife."

The balance between animal and human life is also the theme of his personal life. He made what he calls a life-changing decision while still in college that he would share his time on earth with dogs. From the moment that Niko came into his life, decisions he made were no longer simply personal but oriented to the family of two that they had become. Eventually he came to believe in "pets in pairs"—that no matter how strong an interspecies bond can be, dogs need to be in the company of their own kind.

He created a habitat, and a circle of friends, that nourish and support him, even while he flies from location to location, filming episodes of his Animal Planet television show. He spoke with me just before setting out to film the second season.

· · · · · · · · · ·

OVER THE COURSE of my life I've had about nine or ten dogs—my own dogs, family dogs, or dogs who have lived with me and my roommates. In addition, I was one of those kids who had a zoo in my bedroom and drove my parents crazy. I've been a major geek and animal lover ever since I popped out.

Right now I have two dogs, and I believe that once you get a dog, your life changes. I don't like people who make snap decisions about getting a dog, then one day decide they don't need it any more and that's it, off goes the dog to the pound. If you're going to take on an animal, it's got to be for the life of that animal, and with a dog, it can be fifteen years or more.

During my junior year at Emory, three roommates and I were living in a house in Atlanta with a big backyard. Caroline had a Chow mix named Buddha, and the other roommate and her boyfriend each had a puppy, Sadie, a Rhodesian Ridgeback, and Clyde, a Boxer. Of course, I wanted my own dog. I was thinking about joining the Peace Corps, but I also wanted a dog of my own. I couldn't do both of those things. I couldn't get a dog and then a couple months later go tromping off to a foreign country. If you want to get a dog, you have to make that level of commitment. Your life changes. It has an impact on what you can do and can't do. If I had a dog, I wouldn't be able to join the Peace Corps.

I decided I should adopt, because it's a good thing to do. There are a lot of unwanted pets out there. I started looking around at the shelters. I was over at a friend's place, and his next-door neighbor had a dog that had puppies. These three adorable puppies were peering at me over the fence, and I thought, Oh my God, I've got to have one of them.

The puppies' father was a Husky, and the mom was a little black-and-tan mutt that weighed about forty pounds. One puppy, a boy, looked the most like the mother, kind of like a baby Rottweiler. The other two puppies, a boy and a girl, were black and white. The girl was almost all white, with the blue eyes of her Husky dad. I fell in love at first sight with the third puppy, though, that had big black patches on him, a black mask, and the same brilliant bright blue eyes as his father and sister. And he had his father's curly Husky tail.

I ended up talking to the owner of the mom. She had already promised a friend of hers the pick of the litter. I had to wait a few days till she came to make her choice, and I was worried the whole time: What if she picked the black-and-white boy? I was already bonded with him.

Finally the day came and we went over, and the woman was there with her kids. She was totally into the black and white puppy. She said, "That's the one I want." My heart sank. But her kids said, "No, Mommy, we want this one!" The kids liked the brother, the black and tan one, who was very rambunctious. The sister was a bit shy. The black and white boy was in the middle, a little laid-back, a little interested. That's how I knew he was the one that I wanted. When you pick out a dog, you want the animal that isn't too aggressively playful or super shy, either.

The woman had first dibs. She was really pushing for the black-and-white boy, but her three kids wouldn't go along with it. I was praying, "Please, let the kids win the argument!" and they did. She gave in to her kids. They took the black and tan, and I got the dog I wanted.

I named him Niko, and he integrated with the other dogs at the house pretty well. The other puppies, the Ridgeback and the Boxer, were ten months old. Buddha, the Chow mix, was two.

With my background in wildlife ecology, I've always been fascinated by animal behavior. I learned some interesting things from watching the four dogs in our house interact. It's fascinating to see the dynamics among a pack of dogs and how similar domestic dogs are to wolves. I observed a lot of pack behavior, hierarchies, and the shifts in power with four dogs in the house. In that time period, Buddha, the Chow mix, was definitely the alpha dog. One of the ways that behavior manifested was in stealing toys. If one of the other dogs had something she wanted, she would take it and not let them have it back. She kept them disciplined and in line.

Sadie, the Rhodesian Ridgeback, liked to knock Niko around and drag him around the backyard. Clyde, the Boxer, had not been neutered yet, and Niko was still too young for neutering. At around the time Niko was six months old, the two of them developed this male rivalry. It was interesting to watch—they really got into it a few times. We finally made Eric, my roommate's boyfriend, get Clyde neutered. Then I got Niko neutered as soon as I could.

Because we four humans were only roommates, there was a kind of separation among us. On certain levels, I think the dogs picked up on the internal roommate dynamic. It wasn't that we were constantly fighting, but it's just what happens if you live in a group house. There was a kind of competition. There were always issues of "My dog isn't the dog that chewed up the sofa." "My dog didn't do this or that." As a result, all the dogs in that house felt that they had to protect what was theirs.

As a result, Niko became very food possessive. Not with people. I could stick my hand in his dish, and he wouldn't do a thing. But if another dog tries to eat his food, he gets very surly. It's the same thing with toys.

We all lived another year together before we graduated. Then I moved to Washington, D.C., because I knew I wanted to work in the environmental field. I landed my dream job at the National Wildlife Foundation. I couldn't be more happy. NWF has had this national backyard habitat program since before I was born.

My roommate Caroline moved to D.C. at the same time, and we decided to take a place together. Our choice of where to live is another marker of the way dogs change your life and guide your decisions. We decided not to move into D.C. because we couldn't have room for the dogs. Instead we chose Arlington, an inner suburb with a lot of dog parks. It's a very dog-friendly bastion of liberalness in conservative Virginia. People are really into their dogs. It's one of the things I love about living here.

Around that time Niko was getting older, and feeling mature. He didn't want to be pushed around by Buddha any more. They got into a big fight, and he basically knocked her down from her pedestal. He wanted to let her know it was not an alpha-subordinate relationship any more. It was more a peer relationship.

Around that same time, Niko started another fascinating behavior, which I first noticed at the dog parks. He became very particular about dogs that he likes and doesn't like. And I think this is clearly a result of being beat up on by Clyde the Boxer as a puppy.

Basically, he has this crazy aggression toward Boxers. We went through a phase where he would just attack them on sight. I had to talk him down when we even saw a Boxer in the next block. People don't believe me until they see it. They ask how he can know what kind of dog it is. But he knows. His hackles go up.

It even spread out to encompass all dogs with pushed-in faces that look even a little bit like a Boxer: Bulldogs, Rottweilers, pit bulls—Niko goes after them.

He'll be ten next month, and his aggression has calmed down in the last few years. I know him well enough to control him so that he doesn't get into a fight. Niko is very jealously protective of me. He doesn't like it when other dogs come up to me. He's usually fine, but if it's a dog who's on his list, definitely not. He'll warn them off. Then he hovers around me to make sure no other dog can get close to me. It's endearing in a way. While it's a pain in the butt, it's also a sign of how strong the bond is between us.

A few years ago Caroline and I ended up falling out. It was sad because we had lived together seven years, and we would joke and say, "One more year, and we've got a common-law marriage!"

I looked into buying a place, and I saw that the real-estate prices in D.C. are insane. I ended up lucking out because my parents owned an investment place in New Jersey, where I'm from, that they were selling. They needed to find a new place to buy so they wouldn't get hit with capital-gains tax. I convinced my parents to buy down here, and eventually I found a great house with lots of room for dogs.

Niko never had lived without another dog around. He got a little bit of anxiety and began acting out. He started getting into the trash, which he had never done before. He got through the fence, went roaming the neighborhood, and got picked up by the county animal control. I had to get him out of jail a couple times.

That's when I thought, I think I need to get another dog. It's another thing I believe in: "pets in pairs." There's a social dynamic that happens when you are with your own species. Dogs, like wolves, are social animals. No matter how strong the bond is that you have with your dog, there are ways of communicating and experiencing the world inside the species that can never be replicated with a human. I think having a friend adds a lot of quality to your dog's life. It gives your dog the opportunity to have social interactions with another dog. That was the problem Niko was having.

One day a coworker sent out an e-mail saying that her sister had a dog that she was trying to find a new home for. When I heard it was a black Lab, I thought, This is perfect. Niko loves Labs. He loves to wrestle with them, especially chocolate or black ones. If he sees a Lab, his tail wags, he immediately goes up to it, does his play-bow and invites it to wrestle, where they both stand on their hind legs and push each other around.

This Lab's name was Remington. He was about to turn seven. Niko and I drove out to the Shenandoah Valley, about an hour outside of D.C., and we met Remy. He's your typical Lab—full of energy, adorable, but not too bright. He just Labs around. They seemed to get along well, so I asked, "Can I take Remington out and see how they do?"

Niko is a great trail dog. He can be off leash. He keeps his pace so he's just so far ahead. Then he waits for you to catch up. He doesn't take off and run away. We took Remy out for a hike, and we ended up adopting him.

Remy has a typical Lab tail, which can dent your shin. He uses it like a weapon. I can't have tchotchkes around the house or put a glass of wine on a coffee table. When Remington comes through, everything goes flying at the end of that tail.

Shortly after I got him home, I realized that Remy is *completely* obsessed with playing fetch. I got tennis balls and threw them for him constantly. I ended up getting tennis elbow, repetitive-motion pain. It was awful. But I didn't want to stop throwing the ball for Remy because he loved fetching so much.

Then one of my friends bought me a Chuckit!, this plastic gizmo that you use to pick up and throw a tennis ball. It's the best invention in the world. Number one, you don't get the repetitive-motion pain; number two, you can throw the ball twice as far and exhaust the dog. A dog like Remington will sprint and play fetch until he collapses. And the best part about it is you never have to touch the slimy, dirty tennis ball.

Unfortunately, Remy's obsession with fetching means that he wants nothing to do with other dogs: They can't throw balls. So my plan to get a playmate for Niko kind of backfired. But it ended up solving my problem because they had their doggy communication and interaction. Niko stopped getting in the trash and running away. Even though they don't play with each other, they're buddies. They've lived together about four and half years now.

It's interesting to see how the relationship between Niko and Remington has developed. Remington is full of bluster. He's got one of those really deep barks. His initial reaction to Niko for the first couple weeks was to bark in his face. Niko said, "Uh-uh. I'm alpha."

They had a couple of spats, but you have to let them work things out on their own dog level. If you don't, you're going against nature. They have to establish the hierarchies. Eventually they established that Niko was alpha. And after that everything was fine.

Remington knows not to go near Niko when he's eating. If I'm giving out rawhides, Remington knows that Niko has to have his first. If we do that, they're fine.

The relationship between Niko and Remy developed over the years. As they grew older, they started sharing a dog bed. If one of them is on the best dog bed, the other one can come up and share it. They obviously have come to a point where the hierarchy isn't as much of an issue any more. They can just hang out.

When people realize I'm the guy from Animal Planet, many times they say, "Oh, *Backyard Habitat*, is that like making your yard great for dogs and cats?" I tell them no, it's about wildlife, not about domestic animals. But obviously a lot of people who like wildlife are pet lovers. A lot of people think, "Oh, I have a big dog, I can't have a backyard habitat." That's not true.

It's your responsibility to be in control of your pet and not let your pet have a negative impact on nature and wildlife. Cats should be kept indoors, for example. It's better for them. Cats take an enormous toll on small wildlife. Millions of birds a year are done in by cats.

With dogs, some can be aggressive and predatory. Niko actually killed a bird once. There was nothing I could do; he pounced on it. When you attract wildlife, make sure you are not putting them in a situation where they just get mauled and killed by your pets. For example, you can make sure you have dense shrubs and cover where the birds and animals can run when your dogs are after them.

On the show, we deal a lot with pet issues, particularly in regard to wildlife. There are things people need to know. For instance, the Colorado River Toad is massive, the largest toad in North America. But if you have a dog, don't make a habitat that will attract it. Toads have glands behind their eyes that produce a toxin. The Colorado River Toads are so big that there have been cases where dogs killed them, ate them, or even just mouthed them, and got the poison, and died.

Then there's coyotes. Since we eradicated gray wolves, the only predator of coyotes, coyotes have expanded their land. They are one of the few animals that have expanded their wildlife habitat even in the face of urban development. Coyotes eat small mammals, and domestic cats and dogs are definitely on the menu. And right now, coyote country is every state but Hawaii.

A few years ago, I met a guy named Dale, who lived in North Carolina. We had been dating for just a few months, doing the long-distance thing, when I went down to see him. His friends Susan and Lynn had a Saint Bernard named Orson that Dale was just in love with, and they hooked Dale up with the breeder. The four of us went out to the kennel.

There were three in the litter. One little girl puppy had a scratch on her eye. The breeder had taken her to the vet, but the eye was big and bulgy and swollen. We just fell in love with her, because she had this damaged eye, she was adorable, and she was 50 percent off. Dale named her Hella.

We kind of raised her together. When Dale first moved up to D.C., I wasn't ready to live together, so we had separate houses. Hella integrated well with Niko and Remington. Remington is friendly with other dogs, but his natural instinct is to go up to them and bark in their face. He acts like, "Don't mess with me." But he is completely harmless—all bark and no bite.

Hella figured this out pretty quickly. She was full of piss and vinegar, and she wanted to romp and bite on bigger dogs to get them to play, with those sharp little puppy teeth. She did that once with Niko and he told her, "Uh-uh. You're not gonna bite me." He snapped at her and pushed her down, which is discipline doggy-style. There was never another problem.

Remington, on the other hand, would constantly get all riled up and bark at her, which she just thought was the greatest thing ever. She learned immediately that he wouldn't do anything beyond barking.

So she tortured the hell out of poor Remington, jumping on him, nipping at his paws, constantly going after him. It kind of irritated us, because Remington was constantly barking at her. But Hella integrated, and they ended up being our little pack. We spent all of our time together.

Hella was never alpha to Remington but she could always mess with him because she's bigger. She weighs about 130 pounds now. Remington weighs seventy-eight; Niko is seventy to seventy-five. Hella is just the most adorable dog ever, with all the things that are endearing about one of these big, goofy dogs. She snorts, she belches. She'll eat, and she'll walk away, and go, "Bleh!" And her lips fly out. It's really cute. Her eye never recovered, but she grew up with it, so she was used to it.

When Hella got big enough, Hella and Remington ended up forging this incredible friendship. Remington, as I said, was never into playing with other dogs, but he ended up loving to play with Hella.

When Dale finally moved in with me, Niko didn't like him, and he got protective and jealous of me toward Dale on a couple of occasions, which freaked Dale out. One time Niko was sleeping in bed with me, and Dale came in and leaned over, and Niko kind of growled at him. For me, that's unacceptable behavior, but I understand why it happened. The solution is to not put the dog in that situation again, because he was doing what comes naturally to him.

Dale wanted to hit Niko. He said, "You have to show that dog who's boss."

I said, "No, the dog was protecting me in bed. And you need to understand that Niko is going to be that way, and not lean over me. At the same time, we'll work on making him understand 'Never do that again.'"

The solution was to have Dale develop a relationship with Niko so Niko would not feel threatened by him. And eventually that happened. But Dale still resented Niko, and it was an unspoken bone of contention between us.

While I was traveling for Backyard Habitat, I had to spend a lot of time on the road, and when I'd come home, I'd be exhausted. Dale became responsible for all the paperwork, all the cleaning, and these three big dogs. He is not as much of a dog person as I am, and he couldn't handle all three on a walk. I can go out with all three big dogs, even with them braiding the leashes and getting tangled with each other.

That actually was a big contributor to what ended up breaking us up. We had a different philosophy and attitude in coping with the dogs. Dale didn't understand that dogs need to be dogs and establish their own hierarchies and things like that. And he resent my bond with Niko.

He and Hella moved out about four months after they moved in. My house is small, and having three big dogs was just too much.

There was an interesting dynamic there. He and I coped with breaking up in different ways. It was a mutual thing. We still love each other, but it wasn't working out, so breaking up was for the best. We're going to be friends. And of course, we share the same group of friends, so we see each other all the time whether we want to or not.

Our breakup also impacted the dogs. Dale and Hella are living in a great basement apartment in a house owned by our friends Jeff and Mary. But Hella doesn't have a fenced yard anymore, so she has to stay inside all day. Dale takes her out when he gets home from work, but it's not the same as being outside and rolling in the dirt all the time. So I always say, "Bring Hella over."

Dale needs more space than I do to get over everything. It has impacted Hella because she doesn't get to do as much of that fun doggy stuff that she enjoys. Whenever Dale goes out of town, she comes to stay with us. I enjoy having her around.

After Dale moved in, Niko had to stop sleeping in bed with me. Yet even when Dale and I broke up, Niko respected that he was not allowed in bed any more. It showed me that you *can* teach an old dog new tricks. You've established for the first six years of his life that he sleeps on the bed. Then suddenly you make him adapt to "Only sleep on the dog bed."

Right after Dale and I broke up, I was going through that phase where I was sobbing nonstop. Niko was invited into the bed for a while then because I just needed someone to be there and comfort me. Dogs are really good at that. But he knew that we weren't going back to the way things used to be.

Niko being here, and agreeing to come up and comfort me in bed, lifted my spirits up, along with Remy just being his goofy self. It helped me get over the hump of the breakup. For me, it was my first real long-term relationship. Even though breaking up was a mutual thing, it still sucked. I'm still getting over it.

That's one of the amazing things about dogs. They are there for you. They pick up on your emotions. There is this total unconditional love. My love for animals led me to become an environmentalist, and I hope I'm able to give back to all animals— wild and domesticated—by building habitats for them, and by giving my own dogs back as much love and devotion as they give to me. When I'm at home, on nice days, I can have the doors open and let the dogs go in and out between the house and the backyard as they please. It's perfect. It's the habitat I've created for all of us.

· JUSTIN RUDD ·

QUEEN OF HEARTS

If you trace the history of dogs in society, it's clear

that they have always played a role in developing

the social conscience of man. In earlier times, men

gathered around pens to watch their dogs fight bulls

or other dogs, and the man who owned a dog that could inflict deadly harm was proud. A hundred years later, man wrote down breed standards and invented dog shows, and the man who owned a prize specimen of his breed was proud. Men continue to gather around events that feature dogs—races, national breed specialties, Flyball games,

Frisbee competitions, herding trials, rescue parades, Dachshund Day in New York City's Central Park—and the kinds of events expand every year.

Dog lovers who live in southern California are lucky because Justin Rudd has come up with many unique ways for them to celebrate their canines. Justin looked around his neighborhood and saw an unused beach; he changed the rules in his community so that the beach became a gathering place for people and their dogs. Next came the Bulldog Easter Parade, the Howl'oween Parade, the Haute Dog Poetry Contest, the Bulldog Beauty Contest, Operation Santa Paws, Thirty-Minute Beach Cleanups, and on and on.

Justin founded a community-based social organization that finds ways for people and their dogs to get together and enrich their lives. He is a powerful role model, showing us that making this world a better place for dogs makes the world a better place for all of us. When I spoke to him at his office in Long Beach, he said that his inspiration is his Bulldog, Rosie.

· · · · · · · · · ·

WHEN I WAS growing up in south Alabama, we lived on thirty-six acres out in the country. We would have anywhere from two to ten dogs at a time, whatever would come and eat our scraps. The dogs would sleep in our flowerbeds and chase the horses in the pasture for fun.

I moved to California ten years ago, to a city of half a million people. The population is dense. You can't have a big yard. There's things that you can do in south Alabama that you can't do here in Long Beach.

I wasn't looking for a dog. If I did get one, I wanted a dog I could go running with, like a Lab. But my ex had always wanted a Bulldog. One day he called me at work and said he was going to look at a litter of Bulldog puppies. He called me again and said he had found a special one—could he bring it home?

Of course I fell in love with Rosie at first sight. She was just four months old. So precious. I knew she was the one for me.

Because Rosie's a purebred Bulldog, I know people would love to hijack her if I left her in the yard. So she's an indoor dog. I live in a one-bedroom apartment, and the chair is hers. When I go up to the business district, which is two blocks away, I pull her in a sort of chariot I made behind my bike. It's a red Flyer wagon that has her name on the license plate. I always take her with me. When we're out and about, she really puts smiles on faces. If she's not with me, people stop and ask, "Where's the dog?"

She's a big bundle of joy—all forty-five pounds. I don't want to say she's lazy, but she does sleep a lot. She has a hearty appetite. I think she smiles. I can see it. Some of us dog people can see dogs smile. She sleeps in my bed. Even though she sprawls out, she never takes up too much room. She snores loud. She's generous with her love. She's a kind and gentle dog.

She likes to be around other living creatures. She likes the word "treat" and dislikes the word "bath." She loves peanut butter. She doesn't like loud motorcycles And she hates trash trucks. She knows when the trash truck is coming. She can hear it ten blocks away.

She barks when someone knocks at the door or the doorbell rings. I don't know if it's her way of welcoming the people. She likes a good booty scratch. She likes her cheeks around her ears to be scratched. I'd like to say she likes to have her picture made, but I think it's me who likes to make her picture. I have hundreds and hundreds. Thousands, probably. I haven't counted.

For a few years I lived a block from the beach, and dogs were illegal on the beach. It's not a heavily used beach. So I thought, Why can't I take Rosie there?

I found city codes that would allow a dog on the beach during a special event. I filed for twenty special events over a two-year period. That meant that one Sunday a month, dogs could be on the beach, off leash, in a three-acre area.

Rosie and I would go up there, and we'd spend the afternoon with 400 or 500 dogs. Our attitude was, this is our party, and they are all our invited guests. She still thinks those beach events are for her.

She likes the word "beach" because then she knows where we're going. Even though she's not a swimmer, she wades in the water. She runs in the ocean up to her head, so that her feet are still touching. Then she'll run back and forth—running, not just waltzing. And remember, this is a Bulldog. She runs along the wave line, back and forth. I can only have her there for maybe fifteen minutes at a time for fear of hyperventilating. She gets so excited. I think it's the sound of the waves she loves. Or maybe it's the foam she's after.

From running those beach parties, I got the bug to do other fun things that could include Rosie. They have built upon themselves and grown and grown. I keep expanding the variety of activities because of her.

When I was working in an office, I used to take her to work with me. She would sit under my desk. But now I work from home, and we spend a lot of time together. She sleeps on her chair most of the day, while I'm at my computer. My main job is running my nonprofit group, Community Action Team. Haute Dogs is a part of that. We do beach clean-ups and animal-welfare projects and kid projects and events. Most of my work started at the same time that I got Rosie, about eight years ago.

The other thing that I do is coach women for beauty pageants, like Miss America and Miss USA contestants. I've been coaching women for beauty contests for fifteen years now. It started back when I lived in Alabama. I volunteered for the local Miss America preliminary. Then I started my own preliminaries for Miss USA and Miss Teen USA. After my local girls won the state level and competed nationally, other women started asking me to help them get ready.

I mainly focus on interview skills, and I do some in-my-home coaching, and some telephone coaching. I like beauty contests; I think that's why I started the Bulldog Beauty Contest last year. We had 150 entrants—all English Bulldogs. We're doing it again this year on Mother's Day. Last year we did it on Father's Day. We jokingly say about Bulldogs, "It's a face only a mother could love." I tell people, "I'm the dad of my dog."

Rosie is the queen of the beauty contest, and she knows it. It's kind of a sore point with her that she can't compete. But she sleeps with the organizer, so we can't allow it.

But she's there, sitting on her wagon, which is actually her throne. I tell her, "Rosie, this is your party, and we've invited all your buddies." They parade right in front of her. We have real-life beauty queens as the judges. A lot of them are the women I coach.

Rosie gives a lot of licks to women when they come over here. And I tell them, "Don't pay attention to her, and she'll leave you alone." But they always want to pet her. She loves that, and she always comes back for more. Then she'll get her bone and decide to chew it while we're working. She likes to wedge her bone against their leg so she can get a better grip on it. It's humorous. I always tell them it's good practice. Nothing else can distract you because you're used to Rosie.

The judges are looking for similar things like you'd look for in a real-life beauty contest: figure and form, face and confidence, style, first impression, poise. Then we have alternate categories, like Most Talented and Best Dressed. The dogs can either be dressed or not. We certainly encourage them to put something on to grab the judges' attention.

Last year two of our contestants were Bulldogs who ride skateboards, Tyson, from Huntington Beach, and Darla-Bell, from Pasadena. There's a video of Tyson riding that skateboard going around on the Internet. Darla-Bell was chosen Most talented. We hold an animal-adoption fair in conjunction with the Bulldog Beauty Contest, with dogs and cats and other animals. We try to find homes for the homeless.

The L.A. TV news crews always show up for the Bulldog Beauty Contest, the Easter Parade and the Howl'oween Parade. Our Easter Parade was featured on *The Tonight Show with Jay Leno*.

Every Easter Sunday, at two-thirty in the afternoon, we have more than 500 dogs show up dressed in bonnets and Easter outfits. It started because I wanted to do play-dates at the park. I got a bunch of friends together on a Sunday afternoon at the park, and we were having so much fun with our dogs, I thought we should share it. I said, "Let's go parade down Second Street." It was a spectacle, with fifty of us. People loved it. Everyone wanted to wave at us, and pet the dogs, and take pictures.

So I said, "Let's do it again next month." So we did. Then I said, "Well, Easter's coming up, let's do an Easter parade." I was hoping to get about 100 dogs. Three-hundred and fifty showed up! Now we're in our sixth year.

The Tonight Show found out about our parade and wanted to bring on some contestants. The producer came down and interviewed in my apartment, with the dogs in their outfits. There were eight or nine pairs of us who talked to Jay.

While we were backstage, Rosie knew that there were people out in front of the curtain, so she was anxious to get out there. We were the first of the Easter dogs to come out. When they called for us, she ran out there with lots of energy, and the crowd just went wild.

Rosie wears a pink tutu that is her trademark. I made pink pearls for her out of pink Ping-Pong balls. I spraypainted them pink and strung them with elastic. She has a white cottontail that I put around her nub of a tail. She wore bunny ears instead of a bonnet that year. Jay Leno was very impressed. He said a lot of things to Rosie, but darn if I can remember what. You put her in front of people, she just perks up. Just like a beauty queen. Right, Rosie?

There's some common bond that Bulldog owners seem to have. It's interesting. All of these events get a lot of gay men coming. Long Beach has a large gay population. And they're not afraid to dress up their dog to help raise money for charity.

We see so much creativity in the bonnets and the outfits. Halloween is easy because every pet store in America now has Halloween outfits for dogs. Half the dogs in the parade will have store-bought outfits. But for Easter, there's no place to buy one. It's not easy, making a bonnet for a dog. People really put time and energy into these things.

I do dog photography now, and a dog poetry contest every year. I put together a dog newsletter that goes out every Thursday to 4,500 local dog lovers. And it's all because of her.

When I look at all those things that Rosie brings to my life, I realize that not every dog has the same fortune that she does. I want to be able to give that back to dogs that are in shelters or are part of a rescue group.

I started the Interfaith Blessing of the Animals, which I hold every fall, with 300-something animals getting blessed by various faith leaders—Catholic and Jewish and Muslim and Hindu. Every December I lead a drive called Operation Santa Paws to collect toys and treats for about 4,000 shelter dogs and cats. We deliver to them in the days before Christmas. The idea is to make the dogs happy and healthy and generally more adoptable. We also collect cleaning supplies and beds and collars and leashes and all kinds of stuff for the shelters.

When Rosie and I went home to Alabama, HGTV followed us for a show called *Going Home*. They filmed the whole thirty-minute episode on us going back to Alabama—a city dog going back to the country.

Then she and I were on a show on Animal Planet called *You Lie Like a Dog*, helping to raise money for animal-welfare groups. The concept of the show was, there's one dog and three people who claim to be the owner of the dog. One is the true owner. Three celebrities have to figure out who the real owner is by asking a series of questions. It was fun. Two of them said I was not the real owner. Only one said I was!

Rosie has her own Webpage on my Web site. I've written poetry to her, which I've recited on her behalf at the Haute Dog Poetry Contest. I have videos of her. Each week I feature a different dog from Southern California called "Rosie's Pick of the Litter."

Each year on the Web site, we have an event we call the Rosies. It's like the Oscars. Rosie is the spokeswoman, and we nominate dogs that have appeared in movies. My partner works for Sydney Pollack, the director, who has several Oscars. Rosie and I often go to visit my partner at the office. One day I took an Oscar off the shelf and put it beside Rosie and took some pictures. It looks like she's kissing the Oscar. It's great publicity for the Rosies.

Many gay men don't have children in their life, so they have the time to spend with a dog. They want something or someone stable. Maybe they don't have a partner, or even a good relationship with their parents or brothers or sisters. But a dog is there. They're just your constant companion, your confidante, and your best friend. I think that's what guys are looking for.

I've read many online articles that say that the senior years for a Bulldog are seven plus, and that the typical lifespan is eight to ten. But I know some friends who had a Bulldog for twelve and thirteen years. Rosie's in good health. She had a cancer scare three years ago. They removed a big growth from right under her shoulder. It hasn't grown back. She still runs around well and eats great.

All these events that I founded have continued because of my love for my dog. It is hard work. But at the end of the day, it is such a pleasure to see the smiles on the faces of the people who are coming with their pets. Or on the faces of the people who come to just be spectators.

Not only that, it's the smiles on the faces of the dogs. That's what I see, and that's what I'll always see. Their devotion to us, their spirit, their tenacity touch me so much. I want more dogs. One day, the right time and the right dog will come along. For now, it's just Rosie and me, and we've got something special. Right, Rosie?

EXASPERATING DOGS

· KEVIN ANDERSON ·

THE DOG WHO OUTED ME

Kevin Anderson hated dogs. All his friends knew that. The only person who didn't know was his brother, Jimmy, who invited him to Vermont to climb a mountain. Jimmy's Alaskan Malamute, Sasha, accompanied them on the climb, and his actions changed Kevin's anti-dog attitude forever.

We've all heard of those valiant St. Bernard dogs with the little barrel of whiskey strapped to their collar that rescue people stranded in the Alps. Dogs like Sasha, who Kevin calls the Wooly Mammoth, also operate in the mountains to help lost or endangered climbers. But dogs do so much more work in our society today than most of us realize, from the cadaver dogs who helped find human remains in the ruins of the World Trade Center to bomb- and drug-sniffing dogs to scent-tracking dogs that can help find missing persons.

Dogs today toil in police departments' K-9 corps, but many human volunteers also prepare their dogs for search-and-rescue missions. These dogs must be trained by age two; by age seven their ability to scent begins to fail and they are retired. Drug- and bomb-sniffing dogs must be trained to a particular scent. Most working dogs are trained to a passive alert: The dog sits and points, for example, rather than digging and possibly setting off an explosion or damaging a crime scene.

Kevin Anderson learned one mantra that dog handlers repeat over and over: Trust your dog. Kevin Anderson did, and it changed his life. He told me about it after work in Detroit.

. . . .

WHEN HE CAME back from serving in Iraq for a year, my brother, Jimmy, decided we needed some sort of bonding, brotherly ceremony: On Christmas Eve—a cold day, mind you—he wanted us to climb a profoundly high mountain. The problem was, I lived in the city, wouldn't be caught dead in a pair of hiking boots, had no interest in mountains, and didn't like outdoor air. If I needed to see some green, I ordered lettuce.

And while I was out to all my intimate friends, I was not out to my brother. He still thought of me in the sweet-and- sour terms of our boyhood, when he, the younger brother, would jump on my back and wrestle me to the ground, and I'd wrestle him. It was probably an exchange that meant completely different things to each of us.

We were raised outside of Detroit in a so-called normal family situation: Our father worked at a factory every day and drank on the weekends; our mother drank during the week and yelled at our father on the weekends. Dad died of a heart attack years ago, and neither one of us goes back to see Mom much. Mom never approved of anything I did, and she still doesn't know I'm gay.

Jimmy wasn't gay, so I thought he got along fine with Mom. It surprised me that he didn't want to spend Christmas with her, either.

We really didn't know all that much about each other. He's eleven years younger than I am. And our mother always got between us.

He'd been climbing this mountain in Vermont almost every single day, and he wanted his big brother to join him. And I couldn't say no, partly because I'd been bragging about my physical capabilities. The hospital where I work has a great gym, and I got in the habit of taking lunch at a weird hour so I could have the equipment mostly to myself and not worry about wiping somebody else's sweat off the seat before I sat down.

Then I even bought a multisystem workout bench so I could do leg curls and biceps extensions and lateral pull-downs and power crunches in my spare time. I was lifting regularly, and working on my cardio fitness, so I'd been bragging to him about it. Probably because I was angry that he was in the Reserves and spent a year in Iraq and had all these credits on his side for patriotism and service to the country and generally good behavior that I was never going to have.

My brother's house in Vermont was this cute, gingerbready, Victorian, little-town thing. There was an old wooden rocker on the porch, even though there was snow all around. And all kinds of Christmas wreaths and Christmas decorations and this Santa in a red sleigh and reindeer with noses that were light bulbs that lit up. The whole thing made me wince.

I knocked on the door, and it swung open, and my brother said, "Kevin!" And my heart melted because he's my brother, he'd been in Iraq, and I hadn't seen him in a long time. He chucked me on the shoulder, and I shook his hand. He called, "Patty! Kevin's here!"

And out from the kitchen came his blond, busty, smiling girlfriend. I went over and kissed her on the cheek. She looked me in the eye, and I could see right away—*she knew*.

She was surprised, but she was sympathetic, too. I could see she wasn't some backwoods redneck who was going to give me a lecture about the Bible. She was very warm and shook my hand and gave it this slight pressure, which meant a million things to me. It said, "I know, I know Jimmy doesn't know, I'm not going to say a thing to him, you are welcome, you're his brother, I just don't want Jimmy to be hurt." All this passed through with this one little pressure from her hand.

I realized that the two of us had the same goal in mind. We wanted to get through the weekend making sure that Jimmy had a good time. That was the main thing.

And the next thing that happened has the most meaning for this story: They opened the back door, and this giant thing came bounding in. This gigantic mass of fur was like one of those strange, prehistoric elephants from the Pleistocene Age that I had previously seen only on Dinosaur Discovery Day at the Museum of Natural History in Ann Arbor. Instead of being smooth and gray, it's covered with long, rough hair, and it's called a Wooly Mammoth. This beast was galloping toward me in my brother's house.

It bounded in, and just before it hurdled itself into my groin, Jimmy said, "This is Sasha."

I suddenly realized there was something else about me Jimmy didn't know: I hated dogs. I hated all of them. I hated big ones, I hated small ones. I hated furry ones, I hated smooth ones. I hated ones with big eyes and long noses, and I hated ones with shiny hair and flat noses. I hated all the dogs I had ever come across. As far as I could tell, they were whiny, needy, clingy, sad creatures whose favorite things to do were mount your leg, stick their nose in your genitals, pee on your furniture, demand to be taken out even in cold and rainy weather, and generally make life awful.

So here I was with my little brother, who I was feeling all weepy and sad for, and he had—a dog. And this dog ran straight up to me, and I thought that I was going to get the big schnozz in the genitals, but he stopped an inch short of extreme pain. And he looked up at me and he grinned.

Now this was something new, because previously I did not know that a dog could grin. But the only way I could describe his face is—he grinned. I got this weird feeling that, just like Patty the girlfriend, *this dog knew*. How did he know? Did he care? Was my gayness going to be a problem in dogland?

It had never occurred to me that gayness might be something that a dog didn't like. But I had never seen a dog like this, a gargantuan monolith of the dog world, and maybe his thought processes were different from the Jack Russells and Yorkies and Chihuahuas that my friends own.

So I said to Jimmy, "What kind of dog is that?"

And he said, proudly, as he handed me a beer, "Alaskan Malamute."

I said, "I never heard of an Alaskan Malamute."

Jimmy said, while the dog started bounding around the room, narrowly missing the furniture, that an Alaskan Malamute was a sled dog. And that Eskimos and polar explorers harnessed the dogs to a sled that they pulled through the ice and snow all the way to the North Pole. He said a dog like this was worth its weight in gold in Alaska. And I was kind of impressed.

In the meantime, the Wooly Mammoth was making me really uncomfortable. He put his head on my knee and looked up at me with these big eyes.

Jimmy started telling me how much fun we were going to have on this climb. He'd been going up and down this mountain since he got back from Iraq two months before, though never all the way to the top. But in honor of us brothers being together, he wanted us to go all the way.

Secretly, I groaned, because in my letters to him I had bragged many times about what great physical condition I was in. I told him I was bench-pressing 100 pounds. But what he didn't realize was that I was doing it for nicer-looking pecs and a six-pack of abs and better cut to my calves. He thought I was doing it for physical accomplishment.

We sat around talking, and of course Jimmy asked me if I was seeing anybody. Patty looked at me with an absolute blank look. And I said, well, yes. Jimmy whistled and said, "What's her name? Is she hot? You should bring her up here some time."

I said, "Uh, Stevie."

He started asking me more questions, and then Patty said, "Dinner's served!"

I could've kissed her, because this just wasn't a conversation I wanted to get into with my brother right then.

After dinner Jimmy dressed me. Which, in an odd turn of events, was fun for him and torture for me. He got out this thick, heavy, ugly jacket that you can wear in case the temperature drops to fifty below zero. And he pulled out two pairs of socks—"one for insulation and the other for protection." And worst of all, the boots. I had honestly hoped to pass my entire life without ever wearing a pair of Timberland tough and rugged, tire-treaded size tens. I looked exactly like the Sta-Puf Marshmallow man, stumbling along stepping on little kids and small cars.

The dog was lying on the floor, looking at me with his calm eyes.

The alarm went off at five the next morning, and I smacked it down and ignored it. The door opened, and I thought it was going to be my brother. If he'd have come in there all full of good cheer, I would have popped and told him that I'm gay, I'm not into sports, my gym is a hangout place, I'm a complete fraud, let's forget the whole thing.

But it was the damn dog. He came over to the bed and put his head down and snuffled my hand. And he wouldn't stop. I moved my hand and smacked him to go away. Then I realized that's what he wanted. He thought I was petting him. He came back again—snuffle, snuffle, snuffle—getting real close to me, and when I didn't get up, he leapt up onto the bed, put his head over mine and started giving me these big, wet kisses. I thought I was going to be ill. I said, "OK! OK! OK!"

I stumbled around the room and started to put clothes on. Fortunately I had only drunk half the beer the night before. So when Jimmy whistled, I screamed back, "I'm coming!" Then I realized he wasn't whistling for me but for the dog.

In the kitchen Jimmy was putting a leather harness on the dog. Briefly I imagined a sled, myself riding in it under a blanket, and Jimmy running along behind. But Jimmy said the harness was good to grab in case you fell; the dog could pull you up. Well, maybe he could pull Jimmy up, because he sure as hell better stay away from me.

We got to the mountain. There was a glass-enclosed bulletin board with a notice that read, "Snowshoeing in the Green Mountains is exhilarating, but trips must be well planned as the margin for error on a winter hike is small."

That made me uncomfortable. I read on: "The trail is marked with white blazes, which can be difficult to see against the snow" and "Deep snow may obscure all signs of the trail—maps and a compass are helpful." Great. I left mine at my last Boy Scout meeting.

We strapped on the snowshoes. I could see the trail, and the snow was really hard, so I asked Jimmy, "Do we really need these things?"

And he said, "Yeah, because otherwise you're going to post-hole, and even if you're OK, you make holes in the trail that are bad for other people." I was thinking, I don't see any other people.

We started off. The fresh air was invigorating. It had an intoxicating touch, and the sky had a warm glow, and the trees were outlined in black, like sculptures. I'd never seen this combination of tough and delicate in the city.

Jimmy had already climbed Camel's Hump and Mt. Abraham. He needed to climb this mountain, Mt. Mansfield, to bag his Vermont 4,000-footers. (That's how he talked, mountain-climber talk.)

He said, "We are going to do around five miles, with 2,800 feet of elevation." I had no idea what that meant.

The dog kept bounding along, totally unafraid. Nothing bothered him. He was so beautiful that I could see why my brother liked him. He had the incredible strength you can have with lots of exercise; he was like our guardian, and no matter how far he went, he always came back to check on us; and he had this incredible exuberance. When we saw him looking around for small animals to hunt, we saw his wildness, like at any moment he was going to strip off the veneer of civilization and attack a bear. I thought like that for about twenty minutes.

Then the trail started to go straight up. I thought, How the hell am I going to manage that? We kept struggling onwards and upwards. Always in front of me, I saw this figure of my brother. Sometimes he was struggling, too, because it was hard.

We got to a place called Smuggler's Notch. There's a small shelter there, and some park ranger had written up some more helpful advice: "Stay alert to the dangers of hypothermia and frostbite. Know the signs and how to treat them."

The sun came out, and it was warm on my face, so it didn't look like hypothermia was going to be a problem.

We hung around there looking at the great view. Jimmy said, "Let's pick up the pace."

I wanted to murder him because I thought we had come up this far at a backbreaking, Olympic, Flo-Jo pace.

Then we set off on the Profanity Trail. That made me happy. I imagined all the profanity that had been let loose on this damn trail by people dragged there by brothers or boyfriends. I started reciting profanity in honor of the trail: "Damn! Piss! Fuck! Shit!

Whore! Asshole! Prick! Dickhead! Douchebag!" I tried to think up curse words in French and Spanish, too.

My brother and the dog disappeared up ahead. I just couldn't go fast in those damn snowshoes. I thought if I didn't have the snowshoes on, I could jog for a few minutes and get caught up. The trail was hard as a rock. In fact it seemed to be some sort of cliff I was going along. If I just stayed away from the ledge, I should be OK.

I unstrapped the snowshoes and stuck them into the rucksack on my back. They didn't weigh much, but when I went to walk, it was like I had just taken a hundred pounds off my feet. I started walking real fast, then I broke into a jog, and then—*wham!* I didn't see any goddamn hole, and yet there I was, fallen into a huge hole up to my shoulders. How the hell was I going to get out? I had pretty good upper-body strength, but while I was scratching and wriggling, trying to get my trunk up on the level ground, I realized something else: There was no mountain beneath me. I was on a shelf made of snow and ice that was sticking out from the top of the mountain. I had never seen an avalanche in my life, but it suddenly occurred to me how they happen. Shelves like this form, sticking out of the mountain, and then they crack off and tumble hundreds of feet down, taking all trees and humans and anything else with them. Funny, the things you learn in moments of complete panic.

I was calling out, "Jimmy! Jimmy!" and then I switched to "Help! Help me!" But we hadn't seen another soul. Who would be so crazy as to come out on a Christmas Eve morning to freeze their ass off trying to climb a mountain when they could be home with a warm breakfast?

Who came? The dog. The Wooly Mammoth saw my situation, and he got this really serious look on his face. But instead of bounding up with his usual enthusiasm, he walked very slowly toward me, as if he knew he didn't want to disturb this shelf or we would both die.

When he got to me, he licked my face. I just wanted him to get me out. I grabbed him, and there was that leather harness. He waited till I got a good grip, and then he started backing up, pulling me. It went real slow, because I realized I didn't want to kick around a lot and disturb the shelf. So I stayed still, and even when my body was out and I was flat on the ground, I let him keep pulling me until he thought it was safe. He stopped and put his nose in my face, saying, "Huh? Huh?"

This dog weighed like, ninety pounds. I outweighed him by seventy pounds, and yet he had pulled me off that cliff. Something to think about.

I threw my arms around him and noticed how warm he was. He wasn't even breathing hard. There was still no sign of Jimmy; he was dancing on ahead, not even worried about me. I put on the snowshoes.

I got to the next resting place, which is called Taft Lodge, and there were more warnings: "Those people who are not in great physical condition are advised to turn around and go back now."

Good idea. Only I wasn't sure that I could find my way back. There were lots of turns and places where the trail disappears, and we had crossed over fields. And besides, I wasn't hurt, and my brother was up ahead, and the whole idea was to get to the top. So I went on.

The dog stayed with me, as if he had decided I needed watching. I came to a fork, and it seemed pretty obvious to me I should take the left. I went a couple steps, and the dog barked. He had stopped back at the fork. Then he turned his head and looked up the right fork. It couldn't be more obvious. He was telling me my brother went the other way. So we went that way.

We were so high up that there were beautiful views. That's something you never get over, looking out over beautiful mountains that go on and on, and it's just you and nature.

We went a while longer and I fell again. This time it wasn't so bad, because I had the snowshoes on, but I was beat and it was tough to get up. I felt like I had no strength left. The dog was right there, and he pulled me up. I had to go on; he just wouldn't let me quit.

Finally we got to the top. My brother was in the shelter, gloves off, sitting there, looking warm, steam rising out of his thermos, and he grinned when he saw me stumbling in, and offered me a cup of hot coffee. This warm, steaming, great-smelling cup of civilization. What did I do? I burst into tears.

I was shaking. I couldn't take the cup. I wobbled onto the bench, bawling my eyes out, and I said, "Jimmy, I'm gay."

He said, "*What?*"

I told him again. I told him that I'm not the brother he thought I was, that I've been mean and rotten to him, that I wish I wasn't gay so he wouldn't have to have a gay brother, but I am. While I was talking, the dog started rubbing his body against my knees. I grabbed him like my lifeline.

Jimmy said, "Does Stevie know?"

I said, "It's Stephen, not Stevie. Stephen." I gave a little laugh.

The dog moved over. He started rubbing against my brother's legs. My brother looked uncomfortable. I was thinking it was because of me, and how awful that weekend was going to be. But then he said, no, he was sorry about making me climb the mountain, he only did it because he hoped I would fail. He said that I was always the older brother who could do everything, and he always felt like he couldn't measure up. He said, "I'm sorry. I shouldn't have made you come out here."

I asked him if he was mad that I'm gay. He thought about it. He said, "No, I'm more mad you're a climber."

I told him about the climb, how I almost died and the dog came and rescued me, and we both started petting the Wooly Mammoth, who loved it of course. He sat between us, looking from one to the other with this dopey, happy look on his face.

Then we started feeling the wind, and we decided it was time to go back down. The descent was easy and fun, and we glissaded most of the way. We had no problem following our snowshoe tracks down. We reached the car around two, just as snow was starting to fall.

And I decided, right then, that I had to have a Wooly Mammoth of my own. Jimmy called a couple people, and he figured that if I came back in the summer, there would be some puppies.

After a while, I realized I couldn't have a Wooly Mammoth in my apartment. I started thinking about how the hair would shed and how the shelves behind the bar sometimes wobble if someone starts dancing hard. But I really wanted the Wooly Mammoth. It was a big dilemma.

I talked to Jimmy about it, and he had an idea. We went to see a friend of his who had adopted a Greyhound from a racetrack. This animal was sleek and gorgeous, much quieter than the woolly mammoth. The way he sat around, posing on his pillow, he was more like a work of art than a prehistoric creature. But he had a lot in common with the Wooly Mammoth, including those big eyes that look right inside your soul and see everything.

So I got a Greyhound and named him Lincoln. He is gentle and understanding. I've told him all about the Wooly Mammoth and how he outed me that weekend, but Lincoln is too kind to judge. Next summer I am going to drive him out to my brother's house so he can meet the Wooly Mammoth and have a word with him. Lincoln would never out anybody. He's not that kind of dog.

· EDWARD ALBEE ·

OWNED BY IRISH
WOLFHOUNDS

Edward Albee is one of the world's most re-
nowned playwrights, a three-time Pulitzer Prize winner and the master of bitter dialogue between battling
couples. Audiences have been thrilled by his plays, from the
first, *Zoo Story*, to the three Pulitzer winners, *A Delicate Balance*,
Seascape, and *Three Tall Women*. His best-known work, *Who's
Afraid of Virginia Woolf?*, was made into a thrilling 1966 film
starring Richard Burton and Elizabeth Taylor and nominated
for thirteen Academy Awards, winning five. But only his

close friends know that beyond the sharp pen of the celebrated playwright beats the heart of a true dog lover.

I first met Edward Albee in Miami in 1987, when he gave the keynote speech at the Miami Book Fair. We had gathered to listen to him enlighten us about his creative process, and what most caught my attention was his reference to Irish Wolfhounds: "Man thinks that he is the only species capable of feeling emotion," he said, "but anyone who owns an Irish Wolfhound knows that's not true."

That reference went straight to my heart. All the dog literature I'd read up to that point claimed that dogs didn't have emotions, and that people who said otherwise were guilty of anthropomorphism, the projection of human traits onto animals. Scientists and psychologists discounted the idea that a pet could return the love of its human. They argued that if animals appeared to express emotions, it was merely because they were reacting to hormonal rushes triggered by outside stimuli. An expert recently quoted by the BBC's environmental reporter said that much writing today is, "leading people to suggest animals can feel sensation and emotion in the same way as humans. It is obviously nonsense."

That view contrasts sharply with my observations of my own dogs, who seem to stick with me through genuine affection, and not only because I'm a good provider of meals. These ideas were very much on my mind at the time, so I was thrilled that one of America's most important playwrights was willing to speak about such feelings publicly.

When I introduced myself as an owner and admirer of sighthounds and asked if I could interview him on the subject for the magazine *Sighthound Review*, he responded with an invitation to his home in the lush Miami suburb of Coconut Grove.

I'll never forget walking up to that house. I was nearly trembling with trepidation—this was the famous man who had his characters in *Who's Afraid of Virginia Woolf?* bitterly taunt each other in games called "Get the Guests" and "Humiliate the Hosts." I was certainly not up to a battle of repartee with Edward Albee. There wouldn't be any dogs around to distract us; Albee had already told me that the Irish Wolfhounds were at his home in Montauk.

The house was set in a grove of mature coconut palms, surrounded by ferns, plumeria and cycads; the light that filtered through was a shimmering pale green. It was eight-thirty in the morning. I'm not a morning person, but Albee is. He was dressed in a loose flowered shirt and light tan chinos. In the kitchen, his partner, Jonathan, was making pancakes for two guests wearing beautiful satin dressing gowns. Jonathan offered me breakfast, but I was too nervous to eat.

Edward Albee and I spoke in a bright room in comfortable chairs. I asked how he had become interested in Irish Wolfhounds.

. . . .

I BECAME INTERESTED in Irish Wolfhounds because a friend had one. He was a painter. He had invited me over to look at his canvases, and this dog came up and leaned against me. I sat down to look at a painting, and he sat down and looked with me. We moved out to his studio to look at another painting, and this big dog sat down next to me again. We went to the kitchen to get a cup of coffee, and he stuck to my side. He had this big head, and wherever I sat, he put his head on my knee and looked up at me with his big, dark eyes. We became very good friends. He was the dog that introduced me to Irish Wolfhounds. They are the loveliest of creatures. I decided I had to have one. That was in 1969.

I'd always been a dog lover. Whenever I visit someone who owns a dog, pretty soon the animal of the house has drifted over to sit near me. People are always telling me, "This animal doesn't like anybody—I don't know why he's so taken with you." Animals and I just seem to get along.

I've had as many as three Irish Wolfhounds at a time. The Wolfhound breed is very special to me, but I like all dogs. At one time I had three Irish Wolfhounds, one Lhasa Apso, and one cat. Right now I have one Irish Wolfhound, one Norwegian Elkhound, and two Siamese cats.

Irish Wolfhounds were originally bred to hunt wolves. We don't have a lot of wolves in Montauk, so they're not going after their natural prey. But their hunting nature is always with them. They are indefatigable. They can run forever.

Back when the Romans first came to Ireland, they took some of the early Irish Wolfhounds back to Rome with them and paraded them around. I wanted to parade mine around in New York. I got big leather collars for them. We would go to Central Park and walk to a huge hill. The dogs and I would stand at the top. The hill sloped down before us for about 300 yards. If they saw a squirrel at the bottom of the hill, they would race down it, knocking over people and bicyclists on their way. They just had to chase the squirrel. It was inconvenient for the people, but the dogs loved it.

But now I travel a great deal, so the dogs stay out in Montauk, where they have lots of room. It's not the ideal twelve-months-a-year relationship. I used to bring them with me when I went into New York. They didn't care for living in the city. I couldn't blame them; there's a lot an animal has to put up with: small spaces, lots of traffic, always being on a leash, strange smells, and all the noise. When you think that dogs' ability to smell and hear is many times greater than ours, and hundreds of different smells and sounds are constantly coming at them—I could tell that they were troubled by all that. Being in the city, with its intense civilization, didn't really suit these large creatures. And they like to stretch their legs.

I missed their company, but it was better for them in Montauk. They get to be outside, with lots of fresh air, and grass, and sand to run around on. I take a lot of walks, and they always keep me company. Every day I go down to the post office to pick up the mail, and the dogs get to greet everybody and say hello to their friends.

My current Wolfhound is a lovely girl, Samantha. My first one was Harold, then came Jane, Jennifer, and Andrew. There have been five altogether. I've never had a favorite. I have been deeply touched by all of them. Each one had a distinct personality, with their own likes and dislikes. It was a pleasure to get to know them.

Harold, for example, was the dog that sighed. He lived the longest—twelve years, very old for an Irish Wolfhound. Toward the end he was clearly in great discomfort from terrible arthritis. When I say that he sighed, I don't mean the kind of moans and groans he made when he stood up. I mean the sighs that he made in response to my comments. If we were sitting in Montauk watching the waves, and I asked him if he was happy, he'd look up at me and sigh, and I took that to mean yes, he was happy.

And sometimes I'd see him staring off into the distance, and he'd sigh. Not in response to anything I'd said, just his commentary on his life.

I've gotten each dog from a different breeder. I make my choice on the personality of the puppy: Accessibility—a dog that's not frightened of people. Alert. Sensitive. My Wolfhounds, in particular, have always been thoughtful, generous and intelligent—qualities that really mark the breed.

When I pick a dog, I want one that is both fully an animal, with animal instincts and one that relates to other animals, and one that is fond of being around people. I find that Wolfhounds satisfy both requirements.

Andrew was shown by his breeder, one time, and won a prize. But I'm not really interested in that side of it. I like dogs. I find the bigger they get, the more I like them. I did have the one Lhasa Apso, a small dog, but he had a terrier personality—big.

There is an interesting thing about Samantha: When she was

three or four months old, a piece of cartilage got into her spinal column, and her back legs became paralyzed. We took her to the best vets, but they all shook their heads and said she'd never walk again. Some suggested I put her to sleep, but I couldn't do that because it was clear she enjoyed her life. She was dragging herself around, but she was not in terrible pain.

She was determined to walk again. She kept going, and taught all her muscles how to take over and compensate for this problem. In about a year she had trained herself to walk. She was a brave dog; her motivation was that she wanted to get out and run again. The property's fairly large, and she thinks she has to guard it.

With my friends, the Wolfhounds have always been affectionate and gentle. With friends and also with all other creatures, especially cats. Samantha loves the Siamese cats. I find that most animals can get along together if you start them out right.

Of course, there are problems with Irish Wolfhounds. They take up a lot of space, and that space is magnified if you take into account the sweep of their great, swathing tails, which can clear a table in a second. You can't set a buffet table if there are Wolfhounds around; though they may not place their paws on the table to get a closer look, if there is food at their eye level they'll just naturally assume that food is there for them.

My Wolfhounds have always been fond of fruit; I had a Wolfhound once who was willing to wait patiently for the wild strawberries to ripen, then reach his big head in and eat them.

They are most fond of beds and couches, though they are willing enough to lie by your feet on the floor if directed. They are deeply friendly and make the worst watchdogs; since they have such good manners and gentle natures, they will befriend nearly anyone, including a cat burglar intent on robbing you.

Once I was walking the dogs on the beach in the winter. They ran ahead of me, up to the boulders on the northern side of Montauk Point. I heard them barking, and I thought, "They've caught something." Then I heard a different sound of barking, and I thought, "They've trapped a dog behind the rocks." I said, "Come on, guys, be nice. Leave the dog alone."

It was a seal! Some poor seal had gone behind the rocks, and now he was stuck there. The Labrador Current comes down the coast, and sometimes we get seals on Long Island. They're big, about six feet long, and over 200 pounds.

The dogs were wagging their tails—they were very curious about this seal. The dogs were enjoying the situation more than the seal was. I don't know what would have happened. I didn't let it go to its natural conclusion.

Irish Wolfhounds are not known for their longevity. Their bodies are so large that their hearts have to work extra hard to keep them going. The females don't live as long as the males. They get things wrong with their reproductive systems. My females have lived to seven or eight. It's one of the unfortunate aspects of owning such a big breed—they are not with you as long.

Men say that they are the only species capable of feeling emotion. But anyone who owns an Irish Wolfhound knows that's not true. I should have said, "Anyone who is owned by an Irish Wolfhound." That's closer to the truth. I find them to be very emotional animals. Very sympathetic and understanding. I know there are scientific articles that claim that dogs don't have emotions. But I know my dogs. I know they have feelings and emotions, and no scientific study is going to change my mind.

People ask me if the dogs help me in the creative process, and I'm sure they do. I couldn't tell you exactly how. But they're important to me. I work a lot by walking and thinking things through, and the dogs always come with me.

I like to think I'll always have Irish Wolfhounds around me. I just worry if it's fair to the dogs, since I can't be with them all the time. Samantha is fond of the caretaker in Montauk who looks after her when I'm not there. But I like to think that it's me she really loves. Our relationship is special.

· · · · · · · · · ·

Researching this book was the catalyst that led me to get in touch with Albee again. In the intervening two decades, I had come to an even greater appreciation of his playwrighting talent. I had also thought about the fact that his first play, *Zoo Story*, contains a long vignette about an angry, calculating canine who has a profound effect on one of the main characters. I wondered, *Where in Albee's imagination did this terrible dog come from? Was it an actual experience?* These questions were on my mind as I walked toward the Lesbian and Gay Community Center in New York City's Greenwich Village, where we were to meet.

There couldn't have been more contrast between the shimmering light and tropical foliage of our first visit and the gray skies and narrow, bustling streets of downtown Manhattan. As I walked, I noticed many dogs being walked, sniffing trees and wrought-iron fences. True, they were mostly small breeds, more suited for life in the city, but I was saddened to learn that Albee does not currently have an Irish Wolfhound—or any other breed—to share his life. And I knew that Jonathan, his partner of thirty-five years, had died rather suddenly only a few months before.

· · · · · · · · · ·

I DON'T HAVE any dogs now because I'm too peripatetic and alone since Jonathan died. I live in Montauk and TriBeCa, so I'm going back and forth constantly. And I do lots of other traveling. So it just hasn't been the right time. But I've always been around dogs, ever since I was a child.

My adoptive family had a number of dogs while I was trying to grow up with them: a couple of asthmatic Pekingese, which yapped a lot and either remained in armchairs upstairs or were kept in the crooks of arms, and a St. Bernard who was given no exercise except when I was around. He didn't get to run much or rescue anyone from deep snowdrifts the way one imagines St. Bernards are bred to do. At the family stables, where they kept saddle horses, there were also a couple of very nice Dalmatians.

These last I enjoyed most. My family and I didn't like each other, so we got a divorce. One of the many areas where we really differed was that they treated dogs like objects. I couldn't do that.

Early on, when I was living in Greenwich Village, I had a job delivering telegrams for Western Union. They were mostly death notices for poor people who had died in hospitals or been found in the street. The city always sent the telegrams to the families collect, which was awful because these families didn't have a dollar and fifty cents to pay for it.

One thing I discovered is that all the relatives of poor people who die in city hospitals live on the sixth floor. I always had to walk up six flights. There would be a whole lot of family members living in the same apartment, and they'd all come to the door. The family dog would come too, to see what all the fuss was about. It was a big event to get a telegram.

They were really poor. I felt sorry for them. So I'd tell them, "The city wants you to pay a dollar and fifty cents for this telegram. But if you take it out and write down the information, then hand it back to me and say, 'I don't accept this telegram,' then, you don't have to pay. I have to take it back and not charge you." I usually got a fifty-cent tip out of it.

One of the big problems with that job was dealing with the dogs. I was delivering these telegrams on the Upper West Side. In that area, only Central Park West and Riverside Drive were not slums. All the rest was rooming houses—very tough, working-class neighborhoods.

Many of the landladies in these places had vicious dogs. They would see me coming, wearing my uniform and riding my bike, and they wanted to tear me apart. I couldn't understand it because I had always liked dogs. But eventually I came to see that it was nothing personal—it was their job. These dogs had reputations to live up to: They had to go after a Western Union messenger.

I got a lot of good exercise in that job. But it didn't lead me to hate dogs. I would find it difficult to hate any dog, even a landlady's vicious dog. That's where I got the dog that Jerry talks about in *Zoo Story*.

I do believe that there are those of us who feel incomplete without the company of a dog or two. So who knows? There may be more dogs in my future.

· · · · · · · · · ·

Somewhere, perhaps yet unborn, there may be an Irish wolfhound that will own Edward Albee once again. I sent him a photo of my Irish Wolfhound, Justin. He wrote back, "Your Irish Wolfhound looks super. Don't you think you should give him to me?"

· ALISTAIR MCCARTNEY ·

ON THE IMPOSSIBILITY OF
EXISTING WITHOUT DOGS

Throughout history, dogs have been the companions to ordinary men and women no less than the famous and infamous. George Washington, who crossed Staghounds with Virginia Hounds, is credited with developing the Foxhound. Who can imagine Queen Elizabeth II without her Pembroke Welsh Corgis; F.D.R. without Fala, his Scottish Terrier; L.B.J. without his Beagles, Him and Her? Or, for that matter, Paris Hilton without her Chihuahua,

Tinkerbell; Dorothy without "Toto, too"?

Dogs have a profound effect on us—and not just on our conscious lives, but on our dreams as well. Dream interpretation suggests that a friendly dog is a symbol of a trustworthy relationship, while a wild dog represents a great struggle or unresolved conflict. A barking dog foretells bad news, and a biting dog signifies a quarrelsome companion. A swimming dog, a dog that kills a snake in front of you, a fancy pet dog and a white dog are all good omens.

When we asked budding literary light Alistair McCartney if he had anything to say about the unique bond between man and dog, he replied that the subject was so important to him that he'd written about it extensively in The End of the World Book. We thought it might add a literary dimension to our human-canine understanding if he shared some excerpts from the work. The Australian-born McCartney has a unique talent for pithy comments and unusual insights. His mind wanders from his own family history to the Enlightenment philosopher Descartes, and then on to the German Shepherd mix he shares with his partner, performance artist Tim Miller.

. . . .

ON CHILDHOOD, DOGS, AND DOG BITES

WE HAD A chair in our living room that was brown; this was my father's chair. No one else was allowed to sit on it, except for the family dogs: our first Beagle named Bandit and the second named Cossack.

Both dogs' bellies were so fat they dragged along the threadbare carpet in our hall until their fur had become similarly threadbare.

I was one of seven children, and my father would occasionally get our names confused, and refer to me by one of my brothers' names. At times he would become so confused, he would refer to me by one of the dog's names.

Once my father gave Bandit a bone, and I snatched the bone out from under Bandit's wet snout; he chased me and he sank his teeth into my hand. I could not help it; I was filled with envy.

Unfortunately it seemed I had not learned my lesson. One afternoon, coveting Cossack's nice bone shaped like a bow on a Christmas gift, I once again attempted to steal the family dog's bone. The dog had to chase me a little ways before rescuing his rightful property and biting me, this time on the inside of my left thigh.

ON THE SINISTER NATURE OF CLOWN DOGS

WHEN I WAS eight, a circus came to our neighborhood, pitching the so-called big top in the park at the end of our street. Beside myself, I put on my pair of cherry-red corduroy pants and walked down to take a look. The clowns and roustabouts eyed me.

There was a little white clown dog tied to one of the stakes. He had a ruffle round his neck and was wearing a gold pointy hat. One of the roustabouts stopped whatever it was he was doing, came over, and taking the hat off the dog's tiny head, placed it carefully on my own.

"It looks much better on you," he said.

I bent down to pat the dog, and it immediately sank its two sharp rows of tiny teeth into the inside of my left thigh, tearing the corduroy of my pants, drawing blood, and leaving what was soon to become a lovely green and blue hoop-shaped bruise.

ON PHILOSOPHY AND DOGS

IT IS SAID that Descartes had a great fear of dogs. He turned toward philosophy to dispel this fear and to master it, but it only served to distract him: In his dreams, the presence of dogs was constant; their snarls haunted every corner of his philosophical system.

When Queen Christina invited Descartes to her court to teach philosophy, he accepted, unaware that she was deeply fond of dogs, and did in fact own 173 of them. All over the palace he kept on slipping in pools of the beasts' saliva.

On his third day at court, the queen's favorite, a tiny red Schnauzer named Heartfelt, somehow got a hold of the only copy of *Principles of Philosophy*. Descartes took to bed. Terribly weak, he did not have the strength to shoo away dear little Heartfelt who slept at his feet. The philosopher never recovered from the shock of this incident. He died three weeks later.

Today, if you visit the museum in Stockholm, you can view this copy of *Principles*, which was retrieved from the dog. It is turned to page 172. If you look closely, beyond the words, you can make out tiny teeth marks.

ON MY MOTHER AND WILD DOGS

MY MOTHER HAS come to wish me goodnight. She has long red hair with bits of gray. She whispers into my forearms. I've had a good life, she tells me, with plenty of sleep. Though I could have had more sleep. She laughs, and pads off to her own bed.

In the morning, I leave our pink asbestos house and go off to the factory. There is a rumor going around the factory that my mother has died. I can hear people gossiping about her death over the steady whir of the machines. I take off my hair net and rush home.

My three sisters are there, sitting around the kitchen table. They tell me that yes, it's true: our mother has died. What time did she die? I ask. They believe it was at 8:00am. She knew she was going to die, I tell them. My three sisters nod their heads. I decide to make us all some hard-boiled eggs. I put the eggs in the pot, get the water boiling and set the egg timer for ten minutes.

Sometime later, my sisters raise the issue of who is going to feed the dogs. They have been coming down from the hills to visit my mother every Thursday. I will, I tell them. Are you sure? The dogs are still pretty wild, my sisters say.

ON FRANZ KAFKA AND DOG COLLARS

KAFKA IS NO longer interested in writing such long stories, or on paper. He wants to write only small, small things that can fit on the inside of a dog collar.

ON SAPPHO AND DOG KENNELS

SAPPHO FEELS SOMETHING hot and red lapping at her from within, warm like a dog's tongue, like she is nothing but a dog kennel, which explains the feeling of a studded dog collar constricting her heart.

ON THE LONELINESS OF DOG FOOD

BACK IN THE 1970s, when I was a child, there were always stories in the newspaper about old men who were so poor they could only afford to eat dog food. These stories terrified me; I felt convinced that this was to be my fate. It seemed a natural transition to go from being a lonely little boy to a lonely old man, living on dog food, with nothing but a can opener to keep me company.

ON GOD'S DOGS

DOGS THAT WE are, we lap up the sunset, which is, if you think about it, merely the scraps of the day. We delude ourselves that we are free agents, upright creatures, but from where God is, all humans like to live doggy-style; God simply walks us on incredibly long leashes.

ON GOYA, THE ABYSS AND LITTLE DOGS

GOYA LOOKS DOWN at the first splotch of paint on his brand new palette. It is red-black, coagulated like a soul. The problem, he thinks, is how to keep one's visions from turning into a system?

To clear his head, he decides to take his little dog Stain out for a walk. Normally Stain likes to stay close to his master, but today, for some unknown reason, as soon as Goya lets the dog off the leash, it promptly heads for the abyss. Stricken, Goya calls out: "Come back, Stain!" He drops the leash, and runs off after the dog.

As the painter creeps up to the abyss's crinkled edge, his pumps squeak. He takes them off and tucks them into his coat pocket. The curious little dog has fallen in and is rapidly sinking, accompanied by barking. Goya peers in, and notices that the abyss is sewn out of something sumptuous, like a smoking jacket, but one that is becoming slightly threadbare in places. This close, he can feel the abyss's hot breath on his face. He takes in its odor, like the water in a vase of week-old roses.

For a second Goya considers letting the abyss swallow the little dog: could be good for the painting. But something inside him yelps; he leans over and scoops the frightened dog up, gathering its quaking body into his arms, kissing its wet nose, all the while muttering "Stain, dear Stain!" Breaking one of his rules, he takes from his back trouser pocket a paintbrush, and gives it to the dog to chew on, so as to distract the miniature beast from the vastness of its fear.

ON DISCOURSES ON THE METHOD OF REASONING AND SMALL DOGS

ᔆA GOD-FEARING MAN, Descartes was certain that as soon as he wrote the last sentence of *Discourses on the Method of Reasoning*, God would send down a terrible small dog named Doubt and

Doubt would pant, Doubt would salivate all over the philosopher's lace collar, Doubt would understand the book like no human ever could, Doubt would then devour the book, cover to cover.

To prevent such an alarming event from happening, Descartes— a superstitious man—declined to place a period at the end of the book's last sentence in an attempt to fool God, who Descartes believed to be a stickler when it came to grammar.

ON THE DREAM LIFE OF DOGS

WHEN WE WERE children, we knelt on the living room's threadbare carpet and watched the dog whimper in his sleep. We went into the kitchen, where our mother was peeling potatoes, and asked her what the dog was doing. She told us it was dreaming, and we inquired as to what the dog was dreaming about. Our mother informed us that dogs only dream of one thing, hunting rabbits, and that they always dream exactly the same dream. We did not know whether to pity or envy them. Either way, this was the most pivotal moment for us in the history of dreaming.

ON DREAM POOLS AND DOGS

SOMETIMES MY MOTHER would forget to mop her dreams off the kitchen floor. My father would come into the kitchen and slip in one of her little dream pools. My father would be yelling, and the dog would rush in to lap the dream pool off the linoleum.

The dog grew fat on my mother's dreams.

ON MUZZLES, BOYS, AND DOG

WHEN I WAS a boy, riding my bike in the semi-dark, muzzled dogs asked too much of me.

ON ALEXANDER THE GREAT, ARISTOTLE, SODOMY AND DOGS

WHEN SIXTEEN-YEAR-OLD ALEXANDER the Great would make love to his teacher Aristotle, he would do so roughly, forcing his way in with only a bit of saliva. He liked to hear rationality yelping like a dog.

Sometimes, Aristotle dreams that he is a rabid dog called Aristotle, ideas foaming out of the corners of his mouth, and that Alexander is his master, to whom he is deeply loyal.

ON THE GREAT PLAGUE AND DOG'S SALIVA

IN THE FOURTEENTH century during the so called great mortality, King Georg IV, having heard that dog's saliva could protect you, allowed the palace's dogs to pant and drool all over him. He took baths full of the thick clear stuff.

Unfortunately this proved to no avail, and the young King eventually succumbed to the plague. The sores first appeared on his knees; self-conscious, he immediately ordered hemlines to be lowered four inches by royal decree.

ON DOG LEASHES AND THE END OF THE WORLD

THE NOISE THE world made as it ended was very loud, but very brief, like God clearing his throat. The dogs would not stop barking, so we patted them and gave them some treats. Then we took them for a walk without their leashes.

ON FANATICS AND MY DOG

MY BOYFRIEND, TIM, and I have a dog, Frida, who is utterly delightful. She is diminutive and weighs approximately twenty-three pounds. Her fur is a warm reddish-brown and she has a black snout. Her breed is a mystery; a cross between something large and something very small, she looks like a miniature German Shepherd.

Temperamentally, she is somewhat willful and prone to wildness. In the morning, when she greets me, she always has this fervent look in her eyes, that makes me think of the determined desperation of the leader of the 1970s West German terrorist group, the so-called Red Army Faction, Ulrike Meinhof.

ON THE SUBLIME INEXPLICABLE MYSTERY OF WALKING YOUR DOG

AFTER YET ANOTHER fight, we decided to take a walk. I put our dog on her leash and we set off.

As we wandered around our neighborhood, discussing whether or not we should break up, we stopped to look at a sign that had been stapled to a telegraph pole. Above our heads the telegraph wires crackled and hissed. The sign read, "Missing! Young boy with milky white skin and bright red hair. Looks like a fox."

Puzzled by what we had just read, we stood in that spot for a long time until our dog gently nibbled and licked at our fingers, indicating that we should continue our walk, for to walk together on a warm evening is a great and serious adventure.

ON NIETZSCHE, DOGGY-STYLE AND ORIGINALITY

ALTHOUGH NIETZSCHE LOVES fucking another man doggy-style, the dogs are the orange of orange rinds, the dogs are burning, he realizes that the man who is fucking is guilty of copying (by virtue of the physical fact that he is behind the man being fucked.) The man who is being fucked was there first. He is somehow more original, more infinite.

ON DOG HEIRS

IN THIS PHOTOGRAPH, my mother is standing in the kitchen crying, telling me that Cossack has been put to sleep, he had cancer just like Bandit. She is telling me that when she looks into the future, she sees no barking or fur; Cossack is the end of the McCartney line of Beagles. There will be no heir. Her tears are creating a puddle on the linoleum.

ON RABIES AND DELICACY

AS A BOY, I was deeply interested in the idea of rabies. Once I saw a photograph of a boy my own age who had been bitten by a rabid dog. The boy had been bitten on the inside of his left thigh. The caption stated that a rabid dog would wander great distances to find a boy it could bite. A hint of foam could be seen at the corner of his mouth, delicate as Bruges lace. I was convinced that one day it would be my fate to also be attacked by a rabid dog.

ON RATIONALITY AND DOG TAGS

SOMETIMES DESCARTES DREAMS he is wearing a studded dog collar with his name, Rene Descartes, engraved on a metal disk hanging from the collar.

ON THE THIRST OF HUMANS VS. THE THIRST OF DOG

WHEN MY BOYFRIEND is watering the garden, our dog, Frida, likes to come up and drink the gush of water directly from the hose. Her small pink tongue laps away. In my dreams, I am watering, and she comes up to me, to lap up the water directly. It seems that like mine, her thirst cannot be quenched so easily.

ON GIVING WINGS TO DOGS

EACH NIGHT I hack off my wings with a meat cleaver. I fry them and feed them to the dogs, waiting for them to cool so they don't scald their tongues. They eat up everything, even the tough wing-frames.

ON DEATH BEDS AND DOGS

ON HIS DEATH bed Descartes offered no last words, but a last bark, yelping like one of the dogs he feared. Descartes knew that although he had consciousness of the inevitability of his own death, in every other respect he was profoundly doglike; the fear that gripped him in the knowledge of his own death was dog collar–like. In fact he was more of a dog than most dogs, nothing but a canine with a scrap of consciousness. Let us bark in the face of death! He had nothing to offer but saliva when confronted with the world's calm indifference.

ON DOGS' PREDICTING ONE'S OWN DEATH

LATELY, MINDFUL OF the story of Xanthus, the horse of Achilles, who was said to have predicted the legendary warrior's death after being scolded by his master, and all too aware that just like Achilles, I will never be deathless, I have taken to not disciplining our dog Frida.

ON THE SORROW OF PUTTING A DOG TO SLEEP

WHEN MY BOYFRIEND, Tim, and I put our last dog, Buddy, to sleep, it was dreadful. As the nurse injected him beneath the fur, we gnashed and wailed like we were in the Old Testament. Afterwards we took off his red collar and placed it on a shelf.

That night I dreamed of the mechanical dog I had as a child, which yapped and walked. In the dream, I was putting this dog to sleep. I was giving the injection, and I was similarly grief-stricken. Real tears fell onto its fake yellow fur.

ON WASHING ANGELS AND DOGS

DURING THE COURSE of the angel's visitation I detected a foul smell coming from the direction of the angel. At first I thought it must be the angel's breath; but after careful consideration, I deduced that the rank odor was coming from the angel's wings, which looked like they had not been washed for ages. Now that heaven is no longer a place, the angels are homeless.

My dog Frida barged into the room, snout-first. She hates being left out of things. Standing up on her hind legs, she pawed at the angel's creamy muscular thighs with her sharp nails, which were in need of a good trim: a tiny trickle of blood appeared on the angel's skin. I noticed that Frida was also smelling a little fruity. If it is warm tomorrow, I thought to myself, I will wash my dog and the angel.

ON TO BE HUMAN ONE MUST BE A DOG

I HAVE FOUND that to learn to be human, I must avoid all contact with humans, and look toward dogs.

· BRIAN McCORMICK ·

AN UNEXPECTED
CHRISTMAS GIFT

Many people believe that our dogs come into our

lives for a reason. Though we may not know that

we need love, companionship, faith, or just to be

needed, our dogs know, and they fulfill that need. Brian
McCormick's two dogs came into his life in very different
ways, and yet both are equally loved.

The abandoned dog provides unique challenges to the
human who gives such a dog a home. We can never know
what pain that dog experienced—physical abuse, perhaps,

and certainly the emotional pain of being cast aside. Much more so than a dog adopted directly from a mother's loving care, the abandoned dog needs special attention, socialization, and love.

Many resources exist in books and online, answering questions about how to approach an abandoned dog, how to integrate an animal guest into your household, and the many ways to help the staggering number of dogs abandoned each year.

Psychologist Carl Jung taught that every human contains within his or her consciousness dozens of archetypes. "The Abandoned Child" is an archetype that stirs our sympathy and produces the urge to protect. Maybe it was that archetype that moved Brian McCormick to an extraordinary act of kindness one Christmas Eve. He knew he risked the anger of his husband and the resentment of his first adopted dog, but something made him reach out and care for a Boxer who had no other friend in the world. With his busy life as managing director of a dance company, professor to media-studies graduate students, and editor of the *Gay City News* arts section, the last thing he needed was another dog.

· · · · · · · · · ·

FOR FOURTEEN YEARS I worked in the corporate world: information strategy, business analysis, and systems testing and training. I didn't want a dog. When I stopped doing that an d moved to Brooklyn, we got a really big place. My husband, Nick, was traveling a lot, and he wasn't that thrilled with the idea of getting a dog, but I told him, "I don't want to spend all this time by myself." So he had to agree.

In the fall of 1999, I asked around at the New School, where I was teaching, and another faculty member sent me a flyer with a picture of a big, hunky-looking dog. The minute I saw it, I knew this was the right dog for me. I made an appointment to see him.

Homer had been found wandering the streets in Washington

Heights. The people tried to find his owner, but eventually they concluded that someone had let him go. After I knew him for a while, I could see why: He was not an easy dog to live with. He is half pit bull and half Greater Swiss Mountain Dog, over sixty pounds.

I went to meet him and took him for a walk. My hunch was right; he was the dog for me.

Everyone is scared of Homer, but he is a total sweetheart. He's the typical big dog that is afraid of little dogs.

The first three months were total hell. We couldn't leave him alone because he freaked out. We tried to do the crate thing, but he peed in it. He chewed up everything. He ate shoes. Every time I went to put on a pair of shoes, the backs were ripped out.

Then, he ate the arm off a leather couch. I let him have it. I yelled and screamed and told him, "It's over! That's it! Enough! You have to find a new home." He felt terrible. He hid behind a chair and just peeked out at me with his eyes real wide. I'd never yelled at him like that before.

Ever since then he has been the most amazing dog—never does anything wrong. The irony is, Homer ended up getting the best of the whole couch situation. We had to replace the couch he ate. We took it out and bought another one, but when we tried to bring the new one in, it didn't fit. So we had to leave it downstairs in his room, and now he's the only one who uses it. It's a sofa bed. He likes to stretch out on it.

Homer doesn't like to be left alone. We left him in a kennel once for a weekend, and he completely freaked out. So now we plan our vacations around him. We only go places where we can take him.

Two summers ago, when I got a job at a dance festival in North Carolina, he came with me. It was the first time I took him away with me, and he was great.

Then we took him to Massachusetts, where he became intimately acquainted with a porcupine. He thought, Here's a great animal to chase, he's really slow. When he came out from the bushes, he had fifteen quills hanging off his muzzle. They have a sort of fishhook on the end, so when they go in, they don't come out. He had to have emergency surgery to remove three of them that got far under his skin. He was really sad after that.

Then came a life-changing incident for us, on Christmas Eve morning 2004. Homer and I got up at six to take our walk. He chose to begin the day going up the hill toward Montague Street instead of heading over to Brooklyn Bridge Park, and that was fine with me.

As usual, Homer bypassed the dog run, preferring to do his business along the Promenade. At the top of the hill, by the gate to the run, we saw a dog—a Boxer mix—wearing a black leather collar studded with silver stars, hooked to a heavy gold chain leash that screamed "ghetto."

When we got closer she didn't look so ferocious, tied to the fence with a crappy blue canvas leash. She was looking up and down the street, but whoever she was looking for wasn't there. They had gone and left her here. It was clear they didn't want her anymore. But she didn't know that.

This was not the first time something like this had happened. People figure if they leave their dog at the dog run, someone will take care of it.

We approached her from the other side of the fence. She seemed cautious but not vicious. I tried to give her a treat. She sniffed closely but was too worried to eat it.

Homer gave me an amazed look, like, "What are you doing? Those are my treats!"

The chain around her neck was something like Freddy Krueger would wear. You could kill someone with it. Or lock up your motorcycle. Not the kind of chain that belongs on a scared dog.

Homer was tugging on the leash, and so was an instinct inside me that said, "Just leave."

So we continued with our walk. I got my coffee, and Homer

had his peanut butter cookie, and it was nearly seven as we headed back for the dog run's morning crowd. Surely someone else would deal with the matter of the abandoned dog.

The two-acre dog run is bordered on two sides by buildings of the International Headquarters of the Jehovah's Witnesses. They were arriving two by two, hand in hand, neatly dressed out of a J.C. Penney catalogue. They were rushing toward their cafeteria for breakfast and their morning message.

When we entered the park, she was still there, her ears back, not knowing what to do, looking very pathetic. When she spotted us, she got up and looked at us in a way that seemed hopeful. Then she barked at me, as if she was trying to say something.

This time I wasn't so afraid to go up to her. I untied her from the fence but left the leash and heavy chain attached to her collar. She began to run around. I noticed a scar on her leg. The chain was obviously a great hindrance, so eventually I undid that as well.

Now the other folks and doggies were arriving, and she was having a good old time playing with everyone. We stayed a long while, still hoping that someone else would come along to deal with her. But finally it was time to go. And it was clear there was nothing else to do except take her with us.

Trying to get a hold of this dog was a truly athletic activity. Finally we lured her into the smaller dog run at the rear triangle of the park, and I was able to put on the leash.

She looked at me and her eyes said OK.

At home she proved to be sweet, but with a complete lack of house training. Homer thought this was an unbearable assault to his dignity, to have a dog in the house that didn't stick with the rules. But he was tolerant. By the third walk of the day, she was coming to me at the gate ready to be leashed and go home.

My husband pointed out to me that we didn't need another dog. I agreed with him. All I wanted to do was to keep her through Christmas, two days. After that I would find a home for her or get an adoption agency to take her. "This is just a holiday fostering," I told him.

We both spent so much time looking at the new dog that Homer was a little put off. He couldn't figure out why she was walking around his house and getting his attention and sharing his treats. But even though he didn't like the situation, he accepted it.

Nick and I were trying to figure out what to call her. What do you call a ghetto dog in a spike collar? A Boxer abandoned in a pile of trash? A dog that looked tough and ferocious, but really liked being petted and fussed over?

She immediately started testing the boundaries. I was sitting on the sofa, spending Christmas Eve watching television and eating cheese doodles. She lay next to me. She had decided it was safe to close her eyes and take a nap. Homer came over, politely, to help me eat the cheese doodles, and suddenly this exhausted, sleeping dog was on full alert, baring her teeth and snapping at him.

I put her in her place for that. She had to know right from the start that she was not the dominant bitch in the house. She was a guest. These things were Homer's.

Then she peed on the floor. What a mess. I kept walking to and from the park that first day, giving her plenty of opportunity to do things right. But she kept pushing it. She tried to eat out of Homer's dish instead of her own. Homer stood back and watched, but I stopped her. When we got Homer, his basic issue was that he was not neutered. She was unsocialized; she didn't know how to behave around us. Luckily, I have friends who are dog walkers and dog trainers who kept stopping over that first day and giving advice.

That night we settled on a name: Ruby—feminine but tough. It suited her.

The next morning was Christmas. Homer decided we should go in the opposite direction of the park—he didn't want me to bring home any more abandoned dogs. So we went off to walk through a vacant lot where we'd walked for years. They were on leashes, right beside me, and I noticed that Ruby was walking really close to me, like maybe she was afraid I was going to take her back out and tie her to the fence again.

I don't know when she first stepped on that glass. I looked down and thought, *What is that huge thing sticking out of her paw?* And the next moment I saw blood, lots and lots of blood, gushing from her foot. That glass went through her pad and came out the other side. Imagine your palm being punctured right through by a long strip of sharp glass. I went nuts.

I bent down and tried to hold her foot and stop the bleeding. She stood quietly. It must have hurt like hell, but she didn't react. Finally I picked her up and carried her home, but it's hard to hold a forty-pound bundle in your arms while you're running as fast as you can.

I hit the house screaming. Nick says I'm always annoying in the morning, but this time he was *really* concerned. He was horrified when he saw the blood. The two of us tried to get her upstairs into the bathtub. There was blood everywhere. Very *Pulp Fiction*.

Homer retreated to the bedroom.

After we unsuccessfully tried to wrap her paw with gauze, Nick held Ruby with her paw in a towel while I called the Animal Medical Center to see if they were open on Christmas. Thankfully, they were ready for an emergency.

We drove fast over the Brooklyn Bridge, which looked so strange with no traffic, and parked right in front of the animal hospital on Fifteenth Street in Manhattan.

We told the vet, "We don't know anything about this dog. She had no rabies tag. We have no idea if she's ever had any shots." They took her into surgery, informing us on the way that we were probably going to be out a month's rent before they got the geyser in Ruby's leg stopped.

That was not a happy Christmas. But Ruby pulled through—

she was tough. We visited her every day in the hospital. We paid for her shots, we paid to spay her, and $1,000 later, she was ours. Our Christmas gift to ourselves.

Homer graciously let her into his comfy life. Ruby turned out to be a flying squirrel chaser, a tree climber, a rabbit and rat killer, and a crazy girl. She's two years old now, a runty forty-pound Boxer mix, but she's the queen of our house. And Homer allows it.

You would think that Homer would be the alpha dog because he was there first, but she's definitely the alpha. They have an agreement: He doesn't kill her, and she doesn't kill him.

She has chosen Homer's best-friend pack for her friends. Other dogs, even Homer's other friends, she hates. She's very exclusive. We have to leave the dog run at Prospect Park when certain dogs show up. When she's out in the wild, she's totally different. Then any dog is fine. She's too busy chasing squirrels to bother with them. But the dog run—that's her territory.

Homer is the steady guy, someone you can count on to be there. As a friend put it, people want Homer to like them, not out of fear, but because of his sweet personality, his attentiveness, his need for affection. He is also the kind of dog that gets invited to Thanksgiving at neighbors' houses even when they've put their dogs away for the day. He knows not to eat off the coffee table.

Homer and I are so close that I imagined at one point I would want to clone him. But then an op-ed piece ran in *The New York Times* by a guy considering cloning his dog, who just happened to be named Homer, too. He talked about how their relationship was really their experiences together, so that even if the dog looked exactly the same and had the same DNA, it wouldn't be the same dog. Knowing my Homer the way I do, I was pretty convinced that would be the same for us.

He is the only one that I rescued from Washington Heights, brought to Brooklyn Heights, Massachusetts, Vermont, North Carolina, Virginia, Long Island, Pennsylvania, upstate New York, and Fire Island; the only one who spent summers with Robert, Trevor, Erik, Jeff and Tracy; the only one who nearly got us kicked out of the building just for being "a pit bull" (don't get me started). And then there's the scar over his right eye, the one he came with—which the clone wouldn't have. No, Homer is quite clonable, as it were, but he's a unique part of me that I came to see could never be repeated.

And Ruby, well, you'd be crazy to clone her, unless it was for military purposes.

· STEPHEN KWIELCHEK ·

MY PH.D. IN DACHSHUNDS

No matter how strong the emotional connection between a man and his dog, both have to survive the dog lover's biggest challenge—housebreaking.

Problems with housetraining are the main reason that dogs get turned into animal shelters. This basic and necessary step in a dog's life has spawned thousands of experts who have written thousands of books about how to do it successfully. But no matter how successful, there are always a few stumbles along the way.

One big roadblock can be convincing a male dog to inhibit his instinct to "mark" his territory. It is an ancient impulse, brought on by the need to communicate to other males that this piece of the planet is his home range, so they had better move on.

Stephen Kwielchek's story is one I entered into many years ago, as I was one of the trainers Stephen mentions. To their credit, neither Stephen nor his partner, John, ever seriously considered the option of getting rid of the difficult Dachshund, Cab. Stephen had observed a close man-dog friendship before, in the life of his father. While he did not have a dog of his own, he recognized the need John had for Cab's company. He was willing to try anything so that they could get along as friends. And it was Stephen who discovered the magic training technique, although totally by accident.

John is a quiet man who didn't wish to put the story of his bond with his dog into words. But before his death from AIDS, Stephen spoke candidly about his efforts to get Cab to accept him.

· · · · · · · · · ·

IN OUR FAMILY, my father was always the one who got the dogs. He went to the pound and brought back a Dachshund. They were always good dogs, but they were always my father's dogs. I didn't pay much attention.

The first time I visited my partner at his house, I met his dog, a big brown dachshund called Cab, short for Taxicab. John was crazy about Cab. He would spend all day taking the dog for walks, throwing the ball for the dog to fetch, and even when he was watching television, the dog would be on the sofa next to him.

The dog was kind of haughty, a snob. He would look you over when you came in. He didn't really care much about me as long as John was there. John was obviously the center of his universe.

The first time I stayed overnight at John's house was a problem for the dog because he was used to sleeping next to John in bed.

With his short legs and tubby body, he couldn't get up on the bed himself, so John kept a stool nearby for him to step up. When I came over, John moved the stool so the dog couldn't get up on the bed. And you didn't need to be an animal communicator to figure out that the dog hated this. He had to sleep on the floor, even though he had a number of big comfortable beds—and toys and dishes and anything else a dog could want. The dog was mad.

After I left, John put the stool back. He came home that night, and Cab had peed on my pillow. This dog was completely housebroken, and the first bad thing he'd ever done in his life was pee on the pillow. John didn't say anything, just changed the bed.

Next time I stayed over, same thing. Cab peed on the pillow after I left. John was shocked.

I stayed over more and more. Sometimes It was easier to go to John's, a farmhouse in the middle of a lot of fir trees, a long driveway going up to it, lots of privacy and room to relax.

The dog started to take a dislike to me. As soon as I would come in the door, I would see the dog's expression change. He would get this hard look in his eyes, like I was the enemy. It was unsettling. And whenever he could, he jumped up on the bed and peed on my pillow.

I suggested that John permanently remove the stool so the dog couldn't get up on the bed. He removed it for about a week. But John has a soft heart. So one day he put the stool back, and as soon as the dog got up on the bed, he peed on the pillow again. And this time it was a fresh pillow. I hadn't even been there. It was like he'd been saving up and waiting

So John called a trainer. She taught us how to housebreak the dog, how to praise him for being outside and yell at him for doing that "bad thing." John did everything she told him to do.

But Cab was already housebroken. He knew all the rules. He was doing it out of jealousy and spite. He didn't want me hanging around with John.

The trainer said that dogs didn't have jealousy and we were just projecting human emotions onto him. He supposedly had other things on his mind, like "Who is the alpha dog?" And "Who is gonna eat first?" Dog things.

Nothing she tried worked.

Next the trainer decided that we had to make the dog like me. So for the next week, John was not allowed to talk to the dog or feed him. I was the one who had to take care of Cab's every need.

The dog figured it out. He *pretended* to like me. He knew I was the only one getting the food out. But underneath I could tell he could barely stand me—he was just putting up with it for John's sake. As soon as I stopped petting him, he ran to John.

After a while, we decided I should move out to a cottage on John's property. So I rented the cottage, and Cab saw me every day. But we still always had this problem: *Cab peed on the pillow.*

We got a clicker, and we tried clicking when he was doing the right thing, like peeing on a tree, and not clicking when he was doing the bad thing, only we couldn't do it when he was peeing on the pillow because he never did it when we were around. He was sneaky about it. Some days he'd pretend he had no problem with me at all. But the next day there it would be, pee on the pillow.

Then suddenly I got some bad news: My father died. It was unexpected. He had a heart attack, they took him to the hospital, and he lasted three days, then he died. It was really hard on my mother. I spent a lot of time with her, trying to help her and get things settled, because I'm an only child and she didn't have anybody else. I was doing everything I could. And the one thing she wanted most of all was to get rid of my father's dog.

I had totally forgotten my father had a dog, so I went to look at him. I found him in his bed in the laundry room at the back of the house. He was an ugly Dachshund mix named Alvin. I talked to him, and he didn't look up, didn't even lift his head. He just looked at me with sad eyes, and I could tell he knew that my father had died. So I felt really bad for the dog.

I talked to John about it, and he told me to bring the dog to our place. That was really generous of him because we didn't think that Cab would be able to take it. He had been an only dog for so long, and he freaked out when John had another human around him.

But Alvin was very old and sad, and it didn't seem right to put him in the pound. And I couldn't see sending him off with anybody else when he was trying to handle all that grief.

We talked to the trainer, and then a behaviorist. We heard from the behaviorist that before introducing another dog we needed to make sure Cab felt secure about his position. We were supposed to make a big fuss over Cab when we brought Alvin in. We were trying to think what we could do that would add up in Cab's mind to "making a big fuss over him."

All he does is eat and sleep. So I bought him some steak. John decided to go all out: He bought him this bed at a tack store in Middleburg that sells imported plaid horse blankets and sterling silver flasks. People who go fox hunting and drink sherry in the morning hang out there.

This bed was a very up-market luxury item. It was so huge that Cab could have shared it with a Weimaraner. It was made from the softest green plaid wool material. The bottom was a warm, soft mattress, and the sides were made out of bolster pillows. If I got locked out of the house, I would have slept in this bed.

Cab ate the steak and investigated the bed. He instantly loved it. He rolled around on his back and rubbed against the bolster pillows. He was one happy dog.

The next day I brought over Alvin. The funny thing about Alvin is that he was always kind of a chipper dog, always happy and up. Just like my father. When my father died, Alvin got sad. A month later, Alvin was still sad. But I'd be sad too if I realized that the only person I had left in the world was me—I am not anybody's version of a good housekeeper.

But he cheered up when he saw there was another dog. We were so scared that Cab would hate him, but for Cab it was love at first sight. He just adored Alvin. He wanted to do everything that Alvin did. Alvin would sniff a tree, then pee on it, and then Cab would sniff the tree and pee on it. They went around the whole yard that way. Alvin had a crummy, old bed my father had bought him, and I put Alvin's bed next to Cab's in the garage.

It looked pretty sad. John wanted me to throw the old thing out. But I could imagine my father making a special trip to Sam's Club to buy it, and I just couldn't toss it. I thought it might still smell like my dad. Most of the time, the two dogs would sleep in Cab's bed. But every once in a while I'd see Alvin in the crummy old one, and I'd imagine he was remembering my dad.

Alvin and Cab hung out together all the time. Alvin was more than ten years old, while Cab was only around four.

When we went to work, we put them both in the garage and they could go in and out of the yard on nice days. Then they could go back through the dog door and get in their beds in the garage.

When we came home, John went in the farmhouse with Cab, and Alvin came to the cottage with me. We both started to think that Alvin was kind of a cool dog.

Cab and Alvin would lie down touching each other. When they went out, it seemed like Alvin was in the lead. And that's how they spent their days. We still couldn't get Cab to stop the bedwetting, but by then John had unloaded a truck's worth of pillowcases from Bed, Bath & Beyond and we just got used to it.

Things went along for another couple months. Then John all of a sudden got sick. I took him to the doctor, and we discovered he had pneumonia, and he had to go into the hospital.

The first night that John was in the hospital, I went in the house, and Cab was there, and when he saw me he made his really hard face. Then he realized that John wasn't with me. Then I fed him. He realized it wasn't any kind of behavior training: John *really* wasn't there. He had to depend on me. So I talked to him a little, then I took Alvin and went to the cottage out back.

I had dinner, and then I heard barking. Cab wanted to come in the cottage. So I let him in, and he and Alvin hung out together. They talked some kind of dog conversation. After a while Cab wanted to leave. I opened the door. He ran out, saw that John wasn't there, and came back.

This went on a couple times. Finally he realized John was not coming home that night. So he settled down at my place and slept. In the morning I looked around. Cab had never been allowed in my place because, figuring what he did every time he got a scent of me, we thought my place would be like one big urinal to him. But he hadn't taken his usual revenge on me for being John's good friend.

The next night when I came home and called the dogs, Alvin came running to me, but there was no sign of Cab. I was worried. He was in the garage, in his bed, just lying there, so sad, like his heart was broken. He just really missed John. And he didn't know what was happening.

After three weeks, John seemed to be going down. His lungs were not clearing up; he was on oxygen all the time. I spent a lot of time with him. Everyone we knew thought it was AIDS, but he wasn't HIV positive. I couldn't worry about what people thought because John had developed a serious infection of the sac encasing his heart. He was on all kinds of antibiotics, then super antibiotics, another one, and another one, and another one. And finally the doctor said, "If this one doesn't work, we're in a lot of trouble, because our arsenal is depleted. This is the best one we've got. This has got to work."

During this time, I was very solicitous of Cab. I bought steak, grilled it, and when he still didn't want to eat it, I fed it to him, out of my hand, in cut up little pieces. I let him stay in the cottage with us every night.

Alvin was great with him, like he was taking care of him. When

I came home from the hospital, I would sit and tell Cab what had happened. I even took one of John's hospital gowns after he'd worn it and put it in Cab's bed. He loved that. He'd sleep on it on his back and put his feet in the air and rub himself trying to get John's smell all over him.

But he just couldn't understand: *Where was John?*

Finally the antibiotics took effect. John started to get better. First he started breathing on his own. Then he ate something. Altogether it was six weeks that John was in the hospital.

I took the day off from work when John was ready to come home. I helped him up the stairs. I laid down next to him, and we just lay there all afternoon.

John started getting better right away. I told him how Cab and I had really bonded.

I'd read all the dog stories so I knew what was supposed to happen next. After a year of peeing on my pillow, Cab was going to realize that I had stuck with him through John's illness. He would see that I'm dependable and loyal, *fidelis eternus*, just like he is; he would come to love me and never pee on my pillow again.

John spent another week in bed, getting better each day. Pretty soon he was up and around. And things started getting back to normal. Then one night the two of us were in bed again, with Cab on the floor.

The next day John went to work. When he came home, he was really tired, so the two of us went up to his bed. We lay down. I didn't even check the pillow, because I knew Cab was *not* going to pee there anymore. But my head touched something cold, and with my hand I felt the wetness.

I could not believe after all we'd been through that Cab would pull that on me. I said to John, "I have read a lot about Dachshunds. I know Dachshunds are stubborn. I know Dachshunds are hard to train. I know Dachshunds are very sensitive to events. I know Dachshunds are scent hounds and care a lot about smells. I practically have a Ph.D. in Dachshunds. But I can't understand this."

I was so angry that I felt like I was going to kill Cab. I hopped up and started screaming at him. I told him what a rotten, filthy dog he was, how he was a bad friend and couldn't be trusted, and how I was going to spend the rest of my days lobbying John to get rid of him. I told him I hoped he died of a terrible, mutilating illness.

John said that I had better stop or he was going to have a relapse.

I had to get out of there. I went downstairs, and Alvin followed me. He was really worried. I didn't know what I was doing—I was just fueled by anger.

I opened the garage door, and there it was, Cab's magnificent bed, that bed he was so goddamn proud of and always curled up in. I went over—and before I even know what I wanted to do, I was peeing in it.

I peed all over it. The more I peed, the happier I felt.

I looked back to the kitchen, and there were Alvin and Cab, standing there. Alvin has this look like, "Uh-oh," like he was the one who had done something wrong.

And Cab just looked amazed, like he couldn't believe what he was seeing. I zipped up, and Cab came over and sniffed his bed. He looked up at me. He sniffed his bed again. He didn't know what to do. He couldn't believe I had just urinated all over his bed.

I said, "See how much you like it." Because I knew the last thing a dog wanted was a dirty bed.

I wasn't mad any more. I should say that I wasn't *pissed off* any more. I was all *pissed out*. I went back upstairs, where John was changing the sheets. I told him what I had done. He laughed, but I was sure he thought I was nuts. We went to bed.

The next morning, I told Cab, "Don't you ever piss in my bed again. This is war. You piss in mine, I'll piss in yours."

Cab listened.

We came home that night, and the bed was clean. I slept in it, then came back the next night—still clean. John and I slept in the bed all week, and nothing happened.

Not only that, when Cab looked at me, the look on his face was different. He used to look at me with contempt. Finally I could swear the look on his face was respect.

That was the golden key. That turned the corner.

I'm not I recommending this as a dog-training exercise. I don't claim to know anything about housebreaking dogs. But on the other hand, has anyone actually tried this? Are there any statistics on it? Has it been studied? Who knows, I may have discovered a foolproof way to change your dog's behavior. I think experts should get busy and document it.

ABOUT THE CONTRIBUTORS

EDWARD ALBEE is a Pulitzer Prize–winning playwright, author of *The Zoo Story, Who's Afraid of Virginia Woolf?*, *A Delicate Balance, Seascape*, and *Three Tall Women*, among many others. He lives in New York City and Montauk, Long Island.

RANDY ALLGAIER is a San Franciscan living with AIDS who has a long history in AIDS advocacy and gay activism. He served on numerous boards, committees and councils, chairing many of them. His love of animals and gay activism combined when he served as president of the Board of Pets Are Wonderful Support (PAWS).

KEVIN ANDERSON is a financial officer for an international health-care corporation based in Detroit. He now lives in London.

VICTOR J. BANIS is a pioneer in writing about the lives of gay men and lesbians. He has published many books, most recently a reissue of his classic *Tales from C.A.M.P.*, three spy spoof novels featuring agent Jackie Holmes and his adventures with Sophie, his saber-toothed white poodle. Banis lives in West Virginia.

STEVE BERMAN writes speculative queer fiction. He has sold nearly seventy short stories and articles, and his young adult novel, *Vintage: A Ghost Story*, will be published by the Haworth Press in spring '07.

CHARLES BUSCH is the author of the award-winning Broadway play, *The Tale of the Allergist's Wife*, and author and star of such plays as *The Lady in Question*, *Red Scare on Sunset*, and *Vampire Lesbians of Sodom*, which ran for five years Off-Broadway. He wrote and starred in the film versions of *Psycho Beach Party* and *Die Mommie Die*, for which he won Best Performance Award at the Sundance Film Festival. In 2003, Mr. Busch received a special Drama Desk Award for career achievement as both performer and playwright.

HAL CAMPBELL lives in the wine-making region of Sonoma County in a home he shares with his newest rescued Beagles, Penny and Millie. He is also the book critic for *We the People*, the LGBT newspaper in northern California. He is currently at work on his first novel.

JONATHAN CAOUETTE is a director, writer, editor, and actor. His film *Tarnation* was an official selection of the Cannes, New York, Sundance and Toronto film festivals and won Best Documentary from the National Society of Film Critics. He lives in New York City with his partner, David Sanin Paz.

J. R. G. DEMARCO lives and writes in Philadelphia and Montréal. Currently a columnist for *X-Factor* magazine, he has also been a columnist for *The Advocate*, *In Touch*, and *Gaysweek*. His essays have been published in anthologies including *Gay Life, Hey, Paisan!, We Are Everywhere, BlackMen WhiteMen,* and *Men's Lives.*

DONALD L. HARDY is a cube wrangler in Silicon Valley by day, actor, writer, and rogue editor by night. His first novel is currently in the editing phase. He lives on his sailboat in Alameda, on San Francisco Bay.

STEPHEN KWIELCHEK was a paralegal in Washington, D.C. He died of AIDS.

ALISTAIR McCARTNEY was born in 1971 in Australia. His writing has appeared in numerous anthologies and journals, including *Fence, The James White Review, FreshMen: New Gay Fiction, Aroused,* and *Wonderlands: Good Gay Travel Writing.* "On the Impossibility of Existing Without Dogs" is excerpted from his first book, *The End of the World Book,* to be published by the University of Wisconsin Press. He lives in Los Angeles with his partner, Tim Miller.

BRIAN McCORMICK is the arts editor of *Gay City News* and managing director of nicholasleichterdance, and teaches media studies at the New School in New York City.

RANDALL McCORMICK is Senior Systems Manager for a printing company in Atlanta. He and his Boxer, Samson, spend their free time outdoors, hiking, camping, and swimming, and collecting antiques. He is a member of the Human Rights Campaign.

DAVID MIZEJEWSKI is manager of the National Wildlife Federation's Backyard Wildlife Habitat program, host of *Backyard Habitat* on Animal Planet, and author of *Attracting Birds, Butterflies and Other Backyard Wildlife*

JACK MORTON is a four-time Emmy Award–winning stylist. He served as the official stylist for ABC during the 1996 Atlanta Olympics and is the owner of Indulgence Salon, in Atlanta, and WrApsody in Blue, in Blue Ridge, Georgia.

RON NYSWANER is the screenwriter of *The Painted Veil*, *Philadelphia*, *Mrs. Soffel*, and many other films. His memoir, *Dark Days, Blue Nights*, was published by Alyson Books in 2004.

G. RUSSELL OVERTON is a historical researcher for a consulting firm in Lansing, Michigan. He has written both fiction and nonfiction and has two novels planned for publication.

MATTHEW PHILLIPS works in a forty-year-old family construction business, and owns and operates a chain of retail stores that include car washes and oil-change centers in Westchester, New York. He lives in New York City with two Brussels Griffons and his partner of ten years, Saul Sayeh.

JAY QUINN is the author of the novel *The Good Neighbor*, published by Alyson Books, as well as the novels *Metes and Bounds* and *Back Where He Started*, in addition to works of nonfiction. He lives Fort Lauderdale, Florida, with his partner and their dogs, Patsy and Hailey.

LEV RAPHAEL escaped university teaching in 1988 after thirteen years to write full-time. Since then, he has published seventeen books in a variety of genres. Winner of a Lambda Book Award among other prizes, he has been featured in three documentaries, and his books have been published in almost a dozen languages His most recent books are *Secret Anniversaries of the Heart* (stories) and *Writing a Jewish Life* (memoir). He recently married his partner in Canada on their twenty-first anniversary. They live in mid-Michigan with two Westies, Kobi and his younger cousin Yuri.

JEFFREY RICKER is a graphic designer for the *Vital Voice* newspaper in St. Louis, and a contributing writer to *Playback:stl* magazine. He lives with his partner, Mike Wallerstein, their three cats, and two dogs.

JUSTIN RUDD is the founder of Haute Dog, which organizes Bulldog Beauty Contest, Howl'oween Parade, Blessing of the Animals, Easter Parade, and other dog-related community events in Long Beach, California, where he lives with his Bulldog, Rosie.

MICHAEL WALLERSTEIN is a senior sales analyst for Tyco Healthcare International, in St. Louis. He earned his B.S. in business at Indiana University—Bloomington and his M.B.A. from Washington University in St. Louis. He lives with his partner, Jeffrey Ricker, their three cats, and two dogs.

ANDY ZEFFER is the author of the novel *Going Down in La-La Land*, a racy romp through the dark and funny sides of Hollywood. He has written for magazines and newspapers such as the *Provincetown Banner*, *New York Blade*, *Washington Blade*, *Southern Voice*, and *The Express*.